GOLF
MISCELLANY

GOLF MISCELLANY

Everything You Always Wanted to Know About Golf

By

Matthew Silverman

Skyhorse Publishing

Skyhorse Publishing books may be purchased in bulk at special discounts for sales promotion, corporate gifts, fundraising, or educational purposes. Special editions can also be created to specifications. For details, contact the Special Sales Department, Skyhorse Publishing, 307 West 36th Street, 11th Floor, New York, NY 10018 or info@skyhorsepublishing.com.

Skyhorse® and Skyhorse Publishing® are registered trademarks of Skyhorse Publishing, Inc.®, a Delaware corporation.

Visit our website at www.skyhorsepublishing.com.

10 9 8 7 6 5 4 3 2 1

Library of Congress Cataloging-in-Publication Data is available on file.

ISBN: 978-1-61608-256-7

Printed in China

*For Salty Golfers, Catskill Hackers, ADK Golfers,
and duffers wherever you find them.*

CONTENTS

INTRODUCTION

Golf is a great game. It embraces history, tradition, rules, integrity, and yes, fun, all while spending a day in the sunshine—though some would argue that sun is optional, especially in the British Isles. Golf discussion and literature can also, at times, be as stiff as a hickory shaft. So from the outset, the aim for this book is to have a little fun. Oh, the questions are of legitimate origin, as are the answers, but the intent is to write it so fans of golf can appreciate it, whether they have been playing the game for a fortnight or a lifetime. The images included in this book include some of the greatest courses in the world as well as the best ones down the street. Snobbery is being left in the Bushwood clubhouse.

Golf is great because you can play alone, but it is more memorable with golfing partners, especially those who have put up with yapping, snapping, and searching for balls on the fringe of the woods and water. Likewise, this effort was not done alone, not with six centuries of golf to choose from—and that's just counting the start of documented golf in the court of Scotland's King James II, who saw fit to ban his country's beloved game. His grandson did the right thing, when it came to golf at least.

I tried to do the right thing by consulting friends who are not only better golfers, but know far more about the game than I ever will. I especially want to thank Todd Kolb and Dave Martin. Pat Chapman at Night Flyer Golf helped teach me about golf's night moves. Bob Buck, founder and executive director of Eastern Amputee Golf Association, was helpful with insight on golfers with disabilities. Much thanks to Keith Allison for his photos from the PGA Tour. My brother, Mark Silverman, provided numerous photos from courses far and near despite my applying a 7-iron to his noggin when he tried to teach me the backswing at age seven. (Sorry!) Equal fraternal credit goes to Mark's twin, Michael Silverman, who provides hospitality whenever I'm in Arizona—as do Scottsdale-dwelling college buddies Dave Bird and Al Gildersleeve.

Generous assistance with photos was provided by J. Peter Martin, the pro and author in residence at the beautiful Whiteface Club in Lake Placid, New York. On the subject of backdrops, these included West-chester Country Club, Rondout Golf Club, Ridgefield Golf Club, the USGA and PGA Museums, not to mention scattered courses in

New York, Connecticut, New Jersey, Pennsylvania, Florida, Arizon. California, Scotland, Ireland, England, France, and elsewhere. And whi! on the subject of locales, for clarity's sake the third major of the year wi' be referred to in this book as the British Open, though the powers tha be go to pains to call it the Open Championship. Images with no photo credit were either taken by the author or are in the public domain.

The book is set up with eighteen main chapters, the number chosen for obvious reasons. Each chapter is of varying length and complexity, just as every course has par threes, fours, and fives. And because a great day on the course always begs for more, the nineteenth chapter is nine more subjects of varying lengths—like sneaking out for another quick nine at the end of the day when the course belongs to those willing to keep playing until last light.

In writing this book I tried to swing true and follow the game's rules, traditions, and history. If I inadvertently hit out of turn or skull one in the wrong direction, all I can do now is shout "Fore!" There is an explanation of that term in the book, along with eighteen other definitions sprinkled in each chapter. Likewise, each chapter includes a "Did You Know?" feature plus a quote about the game.

Many websites were useful in this research, including afrogolf.com, britishgolfmuseum.co.uk, cbssports.com, dsusa.org, ehow.com, espn. com, golf.about.com, golfblogger.com, golf.com, iseekgolf.com, leaderboard.com, masters.com, mocgc.com, njsga.com, officialworldgolf-ranking.com, pdga.com, pga.com, popeofslope.com, scottishgolfhis-tory.net, secretinthedirt.com, standrews.org.uk, thegolfchannel.com, usamateur.org, usga.org, and usopen.com.

Books I consulted included:

Adirondack Courses and *Craig Wood* by J. Peter Martin;

The Augusta National Golf Club by Sam Byrdy;

A Disorderly Compendium of Golf by Lorne Rubenstein and Jeff Neuman;

Golf's Golden Age by Rand Jerris;

Golf's Greatest Championship: The 1960 U.S. Open by Julian I. Graubert;

Just Let Me Play by Charlie Sifford with James Cullo;

Harvey Pennick's *Little Red Book* along with *And If You Play Golf, You're My Friend* (both co-written by Bud Shrake);

The New Why Book of Golf by William C. Kreen;

The Theory and Practice of Gamesmanship by Stephen Potter;

Tiger Woods: A Biography, by Lawrence J. Londino.

Periodicals of particular use included the *Detroit News*, *Duke Chronicle*, *Golf Digest*, *Golf Course Management*, *Golf Magazine*, *Golf Week*, *Met Golfer*, *New York Times*, *The Official Guide to the 2010 Ryder Cup*, *The Sporting News*, and *Sports Illustrated*, plus access to their archived material available on the web. Thanks also to the archives of the National Library of Scotland. This book provided the opportunity to finally get to both the PGA Museum in Port St. Lucie, Florida, and USGA Museum in Far Hills, New Jersey. If you've got more questions, they've got more answers.

Now let's tee it up.

Next up on the tee at Kilspindie off Scotland's beautiful Aberlady Bay. Mind the wind now, laddie.

WHY IS IT
CALLED GOLF?

here's a few answers as to the origin of the name golf. There's the funny answer: "All the other four-letter words were taken." There's the wrong answer: "It stands for Gentleman Only, Ladies Forbidden." The right answer? Well, let's just say it's a game with a little mystery behind it.

The Scots are credited with coming up with the game we know today as golf, but it had nearly as many spellings as it had rules. Older

Scottish writers spelled the word gouff, goiffe, gowf, gowff, gowfe, golph, goff, and gof—the preferred Scottish spelling by Judge Elihu Smails in *Caddyshack*: "They invented the game there, but they call it 'gof' . . . without the 'L' as we do." And someone who received a red jacket from the captain of the links at St. Andrews would know, hmm, hmm? If the good judge existed. But, to borrow another line from the film, let's pretend we're real human beings . . . and look into the name further.

We begin with the *Random House Unabridged Dictionary*. This 2,500-page tome claims to be the first American dictionary to list the dates of entry into the vocabulary. It places the origin of the word "golf" as "1425-75; late Middle English; of uncertain origin." Well, so much for definitive. *The Oxford Dictionary* sheds a little more light on the subject, before further clouding the matter: "Perhaps related to Dutch *kolf* 'club, bat,' used as a term in several Dutch games; *golf*, however, is recorded before these games."

Putting down the big books, and stepping into the world wide web, we find the authoritative-enough-sounding site scottishgolfhistory.net, which says, "The first documented mention of the word 'golf' is in Edinburgh of 6 March 1457, when King James II banned 'ye golf,' in an attempt to encourage archery practice, which was being neglected." The Scottish king's decree against the game is addressed later in this book, but as to the origin of the word, the site states, "Most people believe the old word 'gowfe' was the most common term, pronounced 'gouf.' The Loudoun Gowf Club maintains the tradition of this terminology."

So we tooled over to the Loudoun Gowf Club in southern Scotland— or barring a plane ticket, went to loudoungowfclub.co.uk.

The first question usually asked about Loudoun Gowf Club is why "Gowf Club"? It would appear that the Gowf Field of Loudoun, so called as far back as records are available, was the private golf field of the Campbell family of Loudoun Castle and had been in existence from the early sixteenth

Irish ruins taken in from the tee at Lahinch Golf Club.

century. Golf or "Gowf," (the old Scottish word for golf) has been played on these fields for over 400 years. It is believed that this ground has never at any time been under the plough in all these years. One can therefore appreciate why the turf at Loudoun is unique and probably among the finest of any inland course. Hampden Park, the legendary home of the Scottish national football team, was re-turfed from the rough along the roadside around 1920.

No matter how you spell it, or say it, or see it, no one said golf was going to be without its challenges—as evidenced by Craigelaw and its walls, hills, and white stakes on the southeast coast of Scotland.

Fascinating, but it is sort of an errant shot in the rough when it comes to getting at the answer of why golf is called golf. The idea of hitting sticks with rocks to pass the time probably goes to time immemorial, but the first documented instance can be traced to Egypt in 2,500 B.C.—the same date derived as the starting point for the origins of another stick and ball game: baseball. Historical games deriving from hitting round objects with sticks have also been credited to the Chinese, Dutch, Flemish, French, Germans, Greeks, and the Roman Empire. Let's have another look at the Dutch.

Holland is credited with the first mention of golf in America—like King James II of Scotland two centuries earlier, the term was mentioned in a decree to cease playing the game because it was a disruption. It seems in 1659 in what is now Albany, New York, the Dutch colony had a problem with the game being played in the streets and breaking windows and hitting bystanders. That in itself shows the difference between the game of kolf and golf. *Kolf*, or kolven, was first developed in the thirteenth century and is still played in parts of northern Holland. Kolf is generally played in a confined space, and a version of it is played on ice, making it perhaps more of a cousin to hockey than golf.

While we're talking references, a 1795 book, Sir John Sinclair's *Statistical Account of Scotland*, described golf as inherently different from kolf, showing that even more than two centuries ago, the two games were considered separate. The Scots have generally been credited with developing the concept of knocking the ball into a "hole," which is far different than its European cousins hitting a round object across several miles toward a barrier (even across ice), or a few feet toward a post (as those troublemakers were doing in Dutch Albany).

So at the end of the day, the origin of the term golf falls under what that ten-pound dictionary told us right off: "of undetermined origin." But it is at least reassuring to know that the urge to use a stick to whack a small, hard object is an urge that goes back a long, long way.

Nine holes or 900 years of history, Leeds Castle in Kent is good for both and is relatively close to London.

Did You Know?

"So I Got That Goin' For Me, Which Is Nice"

A line from *Caddyshack* made the American Film Institute's list of 100 greatest movie quotes? It was actually an ad-lib by Bill Murray, a one-time caddy turned actor, playing the role of Carl Spackler, assistant greenskeeper and former pro jock to the Dali Lama himself:

> Cinderella story. Outta nowhere. A former greenskeeper, now, about to become the Masters champion. It looks like a mirac… It's in the hole! It's in the hole! It's in the hole!

Not quite Clarke Gable's fabled line as Rhett Butler, "Frankly, my dear, I don't give a damn," which was AFI's number one quote. But *Caddyshack* did break 100, dialing in at number 92, ahead of Margaret Hamilton as the Wicked Witch of the West in the *Wizard of Oz*: "I'll get you, my pretty, and your little dog too!"

Golf Defined

Aeration

There are few more aggravating moments for a golfer than going out on a perfect day, paying the greens fee, hitting a nice approach shot, and walking up to the green to find that it has been aerated. Aeration is important for golf courses. It is a process in which a machine punches holes and removes the dirt in a given pattern (also called coring). This loosens soil that's been compacted by golfers constantly walking over it, while at the same time opening up growing area and increasing oxygen for the roots. It generally takes a couple of weeks to return to normal. It's great for the grass but it doesn't help anyone's putting to navigate the small Chinese Checker-like holes on the green. And if the course charges full price and doesn't inform you that they are aerating, find a new course to play.

QUOTABLE

"Golf is a game whose aim is to hit a very small ball into a very small hole, with weapons singularly ill-designed for the purpose."

—*Winston Churchill, British Prime Minister*

WHAT'S INSIDE
A GOLF BALL?

The interior of a golf ball helps determine how far a ball will travel and how much control the golfer has over it. And in golf, everything comes down to the ball and how few strokes it takes to make it disappear in a hole. The ongoing evolution of golf technology benefits both pro and amateur... and there are still enough balls finding woods, ponds, and white stakes to keep golf ball manufacturers quite content.

In the sixteenth century, golf balls were made of wood. That didn't really help them travel great distances and it made the golfer get out a whittling knife or call it a day whenever an irretrievable shot was hit. The creation of the featherie ball in the early 1700s changed the game for the better. A featherie was a hand-sewn pouch of animal hide stuffed with boiled chicken or goose feathers. Upon cooling, the feathers expanded and the pouch contracted, creating a compact ball. After stitching up loose spots, it was then painted and punched with the ball-maker's mark and was ready for a round on the links. But you'd be cursing more than your game if you lost your ball. Because of the effort that went into making them, balls were expensive—often costing more than a club—and if a round was played in the rain, there was a decent chance the ball could split open. Talk about a fair-weather game not conducive to the masses. It took a parson to expand the market and the availability of golf.

Rev. Dr. Robert Adams Patterson of St. Andrews was too poor to own a handmade ball, so he experimented with other materials. The Scottish clergyman used gutta percha, the dried sap of the Sapodilla tree, to create the first rubber-like ball in 1848. According to the New York Times, the substance had been wrapped around an idol sent to the clergyman from India. Patterson found that the sap could be made round and smooth by heating it. The gutty could be made with molds, making it far cheaper to produce—and repair—than the featherie. Rubber companies, notably Dunlop, mass produced balls with consistent patterns on each ball to mimic the way that featheries traveled once they'd been nicked up a bit. Hand-crafting soon went the way of the wooden ball.

Next came multi-layered balls, an idea stumbled on by a bored Ohio golfer. In 1898, Coburn Haskell traveled from his home in

Cleveland to Akron for a round of golf with Bertram Work, superintendent of B. F. Goodrich Rubber Company. While waiting for Work to get off work, Haskell wound a long rubber thread into a ball. When he bounced it on the floor, the ball almost hit the ceiling. When Work finally met his friend, he was amazed at Haskell's discovery and suggested he use a cover on his invention. Haskell put a gutty sphere on what became the first wound ball. The ball was universally adopted in 1901 after success at the British and U.S. Opens. The subsequent Haskell Golf Ball Company was the only company legally permitted to produce the patented design for the first 17 years of the twentieth century until Haskell sold the patent. Dimpling made the balls go farther still—simply put, dimpling maximizes lift and minimizes drag. Everyone wanted to get their hands on the new balls since they added up to 50 yards to a shot—and golfers have always been about the distance.

Haskell's one-piece ball was toyed with by manufacturers in the years that followed, but the results were negligible. It did result in balls that sometimes exploded (a compressed air core was prone to expansion). So the golf balls used by Harry Vardon in the early 1900s were similar technologically to the ones used by Bobby Jones in the 1920s, Byron Nelson in the 1940s, Ben Hogan in the 1950s, and Arnold Palmer and Jack Nicklaus in the 1960s. But it all changed in the 1970s with the introduction of the two-piece ball.

The two-piece ball has a solid rubber core and a long-lasting thermoplastic resin cover. This was later improved to a three-piece ball consisting of a plastic cover, rubber thread windings, and a core. The three-piece ball generally has a softer cover, is more expensive, and does not last as long as the two-piece, but pros like them because they provide better feel and control, plus higher spin rates. The average golfer likely won't see much difference in his game, though they will see a difference in price. The best-known three-piece balls can retail for about triple the price of your average two-piece ball. Still, it's a lot cheaper than a featherie and you don't have to worry about sewing it up after a long day on the links.

Though primitive-looking by today's standards, a feather-filled golf ball was just about the most valuable—and expensive—piece of equipment a golfer had two centuries ago.

With Bing Crosby's famous Pro-Am tournament cancelled for the duration of World War II, the Hollywood star and avid golfer donated the balls to the war effort for the valuable rubber within.

Did You Know?

Shooting Baskets

The 2013 U.S. Open marks the 17th USGA championship tournament held at Merion Country Club in its 101 years in Ardmore, Pennsylvania. Yet even with all its history, including Bobby Jones completing his grand slam there in 1930, no one is exactly sure how Merion came to have its signature wicker baskets on each hole on the East Course designed by Hugh Wilson. Several theories make it difficult to pick a definitive origin of the wicker baskets that resemble more of a punching bag than the traditional flagstick. The baskets, painted red for the front nine and orange for the back nine, used to be made by a staffer on premises. Now they are made by a woman whose identity and location are a secret. To make sure no one walks off with the baskets—smaller versions are used on the practice greens and on tables in the dining room—a basket cart takes them in each night. That kind of tender loving care can keep some baskets around for a long time, with some affectionately named for club superintendents. Superintendent Matt Shaffer said that some of the baskets are "old enough to have kids that can vote."

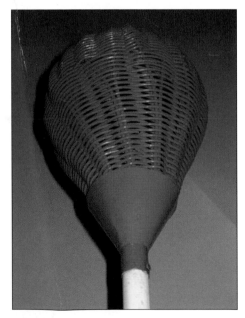

At Merion you don't shoot for the flagstick, you aim at the basket.

Golf Defined

Amateur

An amateur is a golfer who is not paid to play. A golfer is considered an amateur until such time as he or she turns "pro," but amateurism as an ideal dates back well into the nineteenth century. The elite tended to look down on professionals in any sport, before eventually realizing that those who played for money were generally superior to those who played as a hobby. Bobby Jones was the exception. Back when the British and U.S. Opens and Amateurs were considered the "Grand Slam," Jones won all four events in 1930. Jones, a lawyer, then retired as an amateur golfer and became a professional businessman. He created a lucrative series of instructional golf films as well as radio broadcasts. Jones also designed the first matched set of steel-shafted clubs and founded his continuing legacy: Augusta National. As a point of honor, he resigned from the executive committee of the U.S. Golf Association.

QUOTABLE

"It's good sportsmanship to not pick up lost balls while they are still rolling."

—Mark Twain, Author

SHHH! WHY DO YOU HAVE
TO BE SO QUIET WHEN
SOMEONE IS HITTING
A GOLF BALL?

The most critical moments at many sporting events occur at extreme noise decibel levels. Two outs, top of the ninth, bases loaded, full count, and your team's closer is on the mound trying to protect a one-run lead. All 40,000 people in the stands are on their feet, screaming... and if the batter drills the ball in the gap, the place will become as silent as church. Golf is the exact opposite. And that's how people seem to like it.

Golf is quiet, sometimes painfully so during a tense moment. And when the ball rolls in the cup there's an explosion of applause, or, if the ball misses the mark, the loudest noise you will hear is a group "Awwww!"

Golfers all remember when someone made a noise at the wrong instant and a shot was flubbed. Maybe the sound at the wrong moment had little to do with the result, but many an argument on the golf course has happened as a result of someone making noise at the wrong moment and someone taking offense.

The name Danny Noonan is remembered three decades after Michael O'Keefe played the role in *Caddyshack* because of the scene where, with the caddy scholarship on the line, he sinks the putt despite nemesis Tony D'Annunzio (played by Scott Colomby) and members of his entourage repeatedly shouting "Noonan," and variations on that name. So what's so bad about razzing an opponent?

Golf is a game of concentration. It is also a game of etiquette and manners, and nothing is ruder than talking through someone's back-swing—unless that was your phone making its funny little ringtone to indicate you've gotten one more message (or text). As Judge Smails might say as the rest of the foursome, or the foursome playing at an adjacent hole, awaits the switching off of the irksome device: "Well, we're waiting."

Some old line country clubs do not allow members to use cell phones on the grounds at all. When the professionals arrive for a tournament, along with the television networks, the press, and the gallery, it becomes even more imperative to keep the gadgets and the loud talkers at bay. This isn't always easy, but there is a lot at stake. While a shanked drive because of someone's ill-timed ring tone during a

Saturday morning round might cost you a $20 Nassau, the same sin during a tournament could end up costing a golfer his paycheck.

On the 18th hole of round three of the 1960 U.S. Open at Cherry Hills outside Denver, a spectator pulled out a box-style camera and clicked just as leader Mike Souchak was in mid-swing. Author Julian Graubart chronicled the moment in his book, *Golf's Greatest Championship*:

> The shutter's grinding noise startled the golfer, but it was too late for him to abort his swing. As the clubhead tore into the ball, Souchak told himself to just get it across the lake. He skied it to the right and called out in the perpetrator's direction, "You just ruined my shot!" as the ball traveled out of bounds.

Souchak wound up taking a double-bogey six to finish with a 73 for the third round. He still led the tournament by two strokes, but back then the final round was played later the same day. Though trying to dismiss the incident (the offending amateur photographer was escorted from the premises), Souchak wound up shooting a 75 in the afternoon and lost by three strokes as Arnold Palmer claimed the Open with a legendary fourth round. (For more on how Palmer pulled that off, see Chapter 15.)

Professional golfers are individual performers who choose what events to play and are generally not guaranteed any money if they do not perform well. Professional golf is also played mostly at private clubs, where most of the people in attendance would not normally be welcome. Compare that to a large and sometimes publicly-owned venue for most team sports.

Golf is a different game. Even people who find themselves with a ticket to a tournament and don't care a hoot about etiquette or the game itself often get tired of being shooshed or stared at as if they've passed gas in an elevator.

Besides bringing your "indoor voice" to an outdoor event, there are things you should check if you plan on attending a PGA major, professional tournament, or even amateur event. To keep from risking your fancy electronic device's confiscation or taking the shuttle bus back to the parking area to leave it in the car, here is a list of what *not* to bring when watching the pros, as revealed on the U.S. Open ticket order form:

Cell phones (including cell phones with photographic capabilities)

PDAs and/or other portable email devices

Noise-producing electronic devices (including MP3 players)

Cameras and/or camcorders (other than Monday through Wednesday, and without the camera case)

Bags larger than 8 inches wide, high, or deep

Cases and/or covers (such as chair or umbrella covers)

Signs, posters, and/or banners

Televisions and radios unless provided by the USGA

Food and/or beverages

Containers and/or coolers

Pets (other than service animals)

Lawn and/or folding armchairs

Bicycles, ladders and/or step stools or other similar items

Metal-spiked golf shoes

Weapons (regardless of permit)

And any other items deemed unlawful or dangerous by the USGA or security.

Golf can seem like it's no fun to the uninitiated, but keeping mum while someone is hitting—whether it's Phil Mickelson or a plumber from Pocatello—soon becomes second nature on the golf course. It's just part of the game. Hmmm, being outside without the air filled with endless chatter or constantly buzzing electronic devices makes a person long to pick up the clubs and head out to the course. And please, leave the phone turned off or in the car. The world will still be there when you return.

When a golfer goes into his backswing, all should be quiet—and that probably also goes for cameras that make a "click" when a photo is snapped.

Did You Know?

I Believe You're Still Away, General

Golf can get you promoted by Uncle Sam. When Lee Trevino was seventeen, he joined the Marine Corps and spent four years in the service, much of it playing golf with officers and competing in military tournaments in Asia. Trevino claimed that his self-taught golfing prowess helped get him an on-course promotion to lance corporal. The charismatic Trevino, who'd left school at fourteen to become a caddy at Dallas Athletic Club, became a golf pro in El Paso after leaving the Marines. He made it to the PGA Tour at age twenty-seven in 1967, earning *Golf Digest*'s Rookie of the Year and winning the first of his six majors the following June.

As is too often the case on the course, no birdies are in just now.

Golf Defined

Birdie

In the nineteenth century, the term "bird" referred to something excellent. So a shot that qualifies as a birdie generally falls into that level of classification. The USGA gives the date for the adoption of this term as 1899. And if a birdie is good, an "eagle" is better. Birdie came to mean one under par on a hole and an eagle signifying two under. Three under is an albatross, though that rare species is often called a double eagle.

Silence and respect radiate from the clubhouse at North Berwick Golf Club in Scotland.

QUOTABLE

"Golf and sex are about the only things you can enjoy without being good at it."

—Jimmy Demaret, First three-time Masters champion

Measuring closest to the pin on the 15th hole on press day before the 2007 opening of the Pete Dye-designed Pound Ridge Golf Club on the New York-Connecticut border.

WHY WAS GOLF ONCE
BANNED IN SCOTLAND?

Even in its earliest forms golf took time away from the pursuits of productive people. Six centuries ago it wasn't stockbrokers, or lawyers, or even doctors, who stole away to the links on an enticingly pleasant afternoon. Golf was actually deemed harmful to a country's defense. The populace of Scotland was neglecting its archery practice in favor of swinging the sticks.

Being able to pull a bow all the way back and land a shot from hundreds of yards away takes as much practice as landing a long iron shot on a postage stamp green. And if your country is threatened by invasion—and gunpowder is still a relative novelty—it's all the more important to have your archers in shape to fend off invaders. The Scots were ever fearful of invasion or war, since the North Sea separated the Scots from Denmark, Germany, the Netherlands, and France.

But neighboring England was a constant concern and a formidable foe. The reputation of Englishmen with the bow and arrow wasn't limited to the tales of Robin Hood's Merry Men. Bowmen in support of armored knights were England's dominant military tactic in the fifteenth century. British bowman played a crucial role in winning the day against heavy odds for King Henry V against the French in 1415 at the Battle of Agincourt. And if England could cross the channel and defeat powerful France, Scotland had cause to remain ever vigilant. Military training was compulsory for all males over twelve years of age.

So on March 6, 1457, the Scottish King James II's Act of Parliament banned activities that might have a negative effect on military preparedness. The king picked two pursuits by name:

> Ye futebawe and ye golf be uterly cryt done and not usyt And [th]at ye bowe markes be maid at all parochkirks a pair of butts And schuting be usyt ilk Sunday . . . And touchand ye futebaw and ye golf We ordane it to be punyst be ye baronys unlaw. And if he tak it not to be tain be ye kings officars.

Did you get all that? The translation, available through the National Archives of Scotland, states that golf and football (soccer) are henceforth banned, and a pair of targets should be made up at all parish churches and shooting practiced every Sunday. Those still playing these forbidden ball games should be punished by the local barons and, failing that, the King's officers.

Further bans were issued in 1471 and 1491, so obviously these games had not been entirely abandoned if decrees needed repeating. Scotland's elite continued playing golf during the ban. They weren't going to be shooting arrows, so why should they suffer?

James III died in battle defending his throne against rebels, and his son took the crown at age fifteen in 1488. King James IV issued the final ban on golf the year he turned eighteen, but his heart wasn't in it. The young king's interests included dentistry and education—he founded the Royal College of Surgeons in Scotland years before England did the same and introduced compulsory education for the sons of large land-owners. And the man liked his golf. King James IV officially lifted the ban on golf in 1502 and bought his first set of clubs from a Perth bowmaker.

King James IV tried to consolidate the English threat by marrying British King Henry VII's daughter, Margaret Tudor, the year after he rescinded the golf ban. While golf was legal throughout the land, the Treaty of Perpetual Peace with England proved to not be so perpetual when Scotland's alliance with France led to James marching against his brother-in-law, Henry VIII, in 1513.

James was killed soon after at the Battle of Flodden. Though the

battle was noteworthy for its use of early artillery and the billhook—a hooked chopping blade on a long stick—the Battle of Flodden is considered by historians to be among the last major battles decided by the longbow.

Ironic? Sure, but at the end of the day, Scotland isn't known the world over for its archery. And James IV is remembered as "the golfing king," not for double-crossing his brother-in-law.

King James IV lifted the ban on golf in Scotland. It was his breaking of a treaty with England, however, that did in the "the golfing king."

The 12th green faces the rugged Scottish coast at North Berwick, West Links. This true links course plays nine holes with the wind, nine holes against the wind, and sometimes it whips in your face on every hole. Aye.

Did You Know?

Armour Plated and Fearless

Scotsman Tommy Armour served in the British Army as a machine gunner in World War I and rose through the ranks to become a major in the fledgling tank corps. He was twice wounded seriously, losing the use of his left eye in a mustard gas explosion at the Battle of Ypres, and after his tank was later struck by a shell, metal plates were inserted in his left arm and head. Oblivious to pressure on the golf course, Armour left school after the war and concentrated on the game in earnest. Following some success in Europe, he emigrated to America in 1922 and turned pro two years later. The Silver Scott captured the first U.S. Open played at the daunting Oakmont Country Club in 1927. Other notable wins included the 1929 Western Open, 1930 PGA Championship, the 1931 British Open, and three Canadian Opens. A renowned instructor, Armour lives on in the golf clubs still marketed using his name and in his namesake grandson, Tommy Armour III, who won twice on the PGA Tour and now plays on the Champions Tour.

ARMOUR — SNEAD
GOLF COURSE

DEDICATED
DECEMBER 19, 1987

TOMMY ARMOUR
GOLF PROFESSIONAL AT THE
BOCA RATON HOTEL & CLUB
1926 - 1955

TOMMY, BETTER KNOWN AS THE "SILVER
SCOT," TAUGHT, PLAYED, AND DIRECTED
GOLF AT THE BOCA RATON HOTEL
& CLUB.

TOMMY WAS NOT ONLY A GREAT PLAYER
OF THE GAME, BUT A GREAT TEACHER
AND AUTHOR. TOMMY WAS THE FIRST
PROFESSIONAL TO WIN THREE MAJOR
EVENTS, U.S. OPEN 1927, P.G.A.
CHAMPIONSHIP 1930, AND BRITISH
OPEN 1931.

TOMMY IS THE ONLY GOLFER TO RE-
PRESENT BOTH GREAT BRITAIN AND
THE UNITED STATES IN INTERNATIONAL
PLAY AND WON FOR BOTH SIDES.

SAM SNEAD
GOLF PROFESSIONAL AT THE
BOCA RATON HOTEL & CLUB
1956 - 1969

SAM, BETTER KNOWN AS "SLAMMIN
SAM," WILL GO DOWN AS THE GREATEST
PLAYER EVER OF THE GAME. SAM
TAUGHT, PLAYED, AND DIRECTED THE
GOLF OPERATIONS AT THE BOCA RATON
HOTEL & CLUB.

SAM'S TOURNAMENT WINS HAVE SPANNED
A PERIOD OF 44 YEARS, FROM HIS
FIRST WIN THE 1936 WEST VIRGINIA
P.G.A. TO THE 1980 LEGENDS OF GOLF.
SAM'S TOURNAMENT RECORD OF 84
P.G.A. TOUR VICTORIES, 165 TOURNAMENT
WINS IN ALL, AND VARDON TROPHY
WINNER OF 1938, 1949, 1950 AND 1955
ARE RECORDS THAT MAY NEVER BE
EQUALLED.

Boca Raton was home to two of the game's greatest players in Tommy Armour and Sam Snead during a four decade span. The Florida course still bears their name.

Golf Defined

Bogey

The idea of bogey preceded that of par. In the 1890s, when golf clubs, balls, and courses were more difficult to maneuver, the Great Yarmouth Club in Norfolk, England, experimented with the concept of a hypothetical man's perfect score on every hole. The concept invariably became equated with the popular song, "Hush, Hush, Hush, Here Comes the Bogey Man," by Henry Hall, about a creature that frightens children who aren't yet asleep. Chasing around this score on the golf course was like trying to keep away "a bogey man." It was still a few years before the concept of par when, with the proliferation of rubber-cored balls that made scoring easier, bogey came to mean one over par. Just like children learn not to fear the "bogey man," the average golfer comes to accept that bogey isn't the worst thing that can happen on a hard hole. Low handicap golfers, though, still best keep an eye peeled.

QUOTABLE

"Golf always makes me so damned angry."

—*King George V (1865-1936)*

WHY CAN'T YOU GROUND
YOUR CLUB IN THE SAND?

They call them hazards for a reason. And no matter how you look at it, you are in trouble when you are in one. What you don't want to do is make things more difficult by incurring a two-stroke penalty for a rules violation. (You'll want to save any extra strokes—you may end up needing them to get the ball out of the trap.)

The rule: According to Rule 13-4 of the United States Golf Association Rules of Golf, if your ball lands in a hazard there are three things you cannot do:

A. Test the condition of the hazard or any similar hazard;
B. Touch the ground in the hazard or water in the water hazard with your hand or club; or
C. Touch or move loose impediments lying in or touching the hazard.

Grounding means putting your club on the ground behind the ball in preparation of hitting it. Grounding is part of many golfers' pre-shot routines and is within the rules almost anywhere—except in a hazard. (And rest assured that no rule prohibits you from raking the bunker once you're out. Hitting out of the bunker is tough enough for most players without hitting out of someone else's footprint.)

A waste bunker, also called a waste area—or wash—is a different matter. Waste bunkers generally cover a larger area than bunkers and are most often found on links and desert courses. Waste bunkers include things such as rocks, pebbles, shells, and vegetation, not to mention animals who have found a home in these areas often left untended by the maintenance staff. You may ground your club in a waste area without penalty, but many people find it even harder to hit out of a waste bunker than a traditional bunker. Others would argue that case.

But no matter your opinion, you may not ground your club when your ball ends up in a sand trap. The reason is that it may make it easier to hit the ball out, especially since your club will generally leave a mark behind the ball that could act as a guide or make the ball easier to hit. A misinterpretation of this rule cost Dustin Johnson a two-stroke penalty and a chance to win the PGA Championship in 2010.

On the final hole of regulation, Johnson had a one-shot lead following birdies on 16 and 17. A par on 18 meant his first major victory and a bogey put him in a playoff. His tee shot on the 500-yard par 4 finishing hole flew way right of the fairway and came to rest on a sandy patch that had been trampled by spectators. It did not resemble a traditional sand trap and was far from where traditional fairway bunkers would be, but Whistling Straits is like a desert in the middle of Wisconsin. Containing more than 1,000 sand traps of all varieties, the PGA issued a rule to players to treat all sand as if it were a hazard, including those areas outside the ropes that separate the gallery from the golfers.

Johnson grounded his club just before he hit his second shot to the left and well short of the green. He wound up getting on the green with his next shot and barely missed the par putt. Johnson finished with a bogey and, he believed, a spot in a three-way playoff. Moments after he finished, PGA officials informed Johnson of the two-stroke penalty. Johnson would have lost even if he'd made his par putt on 18.

"I never thought I was in a sand trap," a despondent Johnson said after Martin Kaymer defeated Bubba Watson in the two-man playoff. "It never once crossed my mind that I was in a bunker. Obviously, I know the rules of golf and I can't ground my club in a bunker, but that was just one situation I guess. Maybe I should have looked to the rule sheet a little harder."

Johnson's partner in the final twosome, Nick Watney, put the matter of local rules and additional rules sheets in the perspective of the professional. "Honestly, I don't think anyone reads the sheet. We've played hundreds of tournaments. We get a sheet every week. I feel for him. I've never seen fans in a bunker with a player. That was a little odd."

It was odd to lose this way, the first time such a gaffe cost a player a major on the final hole since Robert De Vicenzo signed for a higher score than he shot on the final round of the 1968 Masters, thus missing a playoff with Bob Goalby. (The Argentinean's famous quote: "What a stupid I am.") Johnson felt more stunned than stupid, but Stuart Appleby, who was called on the same rule in 2004 at Whistling Straits, tweeted with enough fury for anyone ever called on this rule. "I'm very pissed and angered that this is the way the PGA came to an end," Appelby wrote via Twitter just after the Johnson's penalty in 2010.

"Never seen patrons walking through the bunkers in any professional event (worldwide). Try that at Augusta."

Try grounding a club in a hazard and someone may call you on it whether you're a pro with the lead at the PGA Championship or a 30-handicap playing in a twilight league at the local municipal course. The name Dustin Johnson will probably come up—and so will your score.

Don't let your club come to rest in a bunker before taking a bunker shot, it could cost you. Just ask Dustin Johnson (right).

Did You Know?

Speed

Clubhead speed for the average golfer is 80 mph upon contact with the ball; the speed is over 100 mph with a driver. Tiger Woods has recorded clubhead speeds of 130 mph and close to 200 mph with his driver. No matter who is swinging, *Popular Mechanics* says that the club maintains contact with the ball for just one millisecond while exerting a force of 660 pounds. Watch that ball go!

Golf Defined

Brassie

This is what used to be known as a 2-wood. Back when woods were made out of, well, wood, this club was the first of the fairway woods to have a brass sole plate to protect the underside of the club from gouges. Unlike a driver, which was designed to be hit off a tee, the 2-wood could get pretty banged up hitting the ball on hard pan or on pebbles—courses a century ago weren't generally as lush as they are today. The brassie did the dirty work.

QUOTABLE

"Golf is so popular simply because it is the best game in the world at which to be bad."

—*A.A. Milne, Author*

An especially nice extraction from a particularly nasty pot bunker on the sixth hole at Muirfield Golf Links in Scotland.

WHY ARE GOLFERS EXPECTED TO CALL FOULS ON THEMSELVES?

If golfers don't call fouls on themselves, the viewers at home will. In the first three weeks of 2011, two PGA golfers were disqualified when television viewers called in and alerted officials to rules infractions after the player had completed a round. While "instant replay" in many other sports requires committees and years of debate to approve of the method, golf welcomes the use of technology in this area, even if it sometimes might make the public wonder why the PGA Tour would want to go to great lengths to penalize its top players—and essentially take prize money out of their pockets. Other sports don't do that—and many of those athletes get paychecks regardless of finish.

That is the difference between golf and other sports. Serious golfers—and certainly professionals—are expected to know every rule, no matter how draconian in its application or consequence. In fact, the USGA *Rules of Golf* states the methodology right on page 1 in the Etiquette Section under "The Spirit of the Game."

> Golf is played, for the most part, without the supervision of a referee or umpire. The game relies on the integrity of the individual to show consideration for other players and abide by the Rules. All players should conduct themselves in a disciplined manner, demonstrating courtesy and sportsmanship at all times, irrespective of how competitive they may be. This is the spirit of the game of golf.

Athletes in other sports aren't generally required to know much more than the bare bones of rules and interpretations. In baseball, for example, players run into sure outs numerous times every season on dropped infield popups, even though the infield fly rules does not require them to run. And in a regular-season overtime game in 2008, Philadelphia Eagles quarterback Donovan McNabb did not realize the game could even end in a tie; McNabb—and many teammates—figured they would just play another quarter. "I've never been a part of a tie," McNabb said after the 13-all final in Cincinnati. "I never even knew that was in the rule book." Consider your sister kissed.

And we're not even taking into account ballplayers trying to fake out umpires with phantom tags or rubbing their arms on close pitches that did not hit them. Imagine if athletes in other sports policed themselves like golfers? If you cheat on the little things, maybe taking performance-enhancing drugs can be rationalized into trying to do what's best for the family. But now we're wading blind into the high grass. Back to the links.

Golfers are expected to call penalties on themselves, even when the infractions are seen by no one else or would have had little bearing on a shot, much less a round. Here are a list of a few recent instances, courtesy of golfblogger.com:

2010: Brian Davis called himself for a two-stroke penalty during a playoff for brushing a reed with his backswing in a hazard. **Result:** Lost in Verizon Heritage Tournament.

2008: J.P. Hayes thought he had earned his PGA Tour card after a solid second round in Q-School (the qualifier for the Tour). While cleaning his bag, Hayes realized he'd played the round with a prototype ball that had not yet been approved by the USGA, rendering the ball illegal. No one else would have known, but Hayes did and alerted officials. **Result:** Lost PGA Tour status.

2007: Brandt Snedeker bent over to pick up a leaf in the rough and his ball moved. He called a penalty on himself. **Result:** Lost Australian Open by one stroke.

2005: Van Houten, a high school sophomore, won the state golf title in Ohio by six strokes. After signing and handing in the scorecards, he realized that one of his playing partners wrote down a wrong score for Houten on a hole. Though the discrepancy was one stroke and still would have given him the Ohio high school title handily, Houten dutifully reported the error and accepted the consequences. **Result:** Disqualification and loss of state title.

Is there a hair golf shirt award for self punishment? No. That is the standard set for golf, especially at its highest level. Like many things in golf, one need only look to Bobby Jones, the greatest amateur the game has known.

Jones called a penalty on himself in the first round of the 1925 U.S. Open when he claimed his club touched the ball ever so slightly. No officials or anyone else saw the ball move. (No instant replay, Tivo, or even TV was around to help people at home make the interpretation for them.) Jones insisted and called the penalty on himself. **Result:** Loss of U.S. Open in 36-hole playoff.

When Jones was asked forever after why he called the penalty when no officials saw fit for an infraction, Jones's reply was simple, and is what golfers still strive for today: "There is only one way to play the game."

Any questions you have on how to play the game are answered in this little book.

A Maxfli on safari.

Did You Know?

No Luck Lighthorse

British-born Harry Cooper posted a record score at the 1936 U.S. Open at Baltusrol, only to have his mark broken a half hour later by Tony Manero, whose 282 for the tournament beat Cooper by two strokes. It was one of several near misses in the career of Lighthorse Harry, who had 20 top 10 finishes in majors but never won; he did win the 1934 Western Open, which was at the time unofficially considered a major championship. His 31 PGA Tour victories, however, were the most by a foreign-born player until Vijay Singh surpassed it in 2008. Cooper became one of the preeminent teachers in the United States, teaching well into his 90s. Lighthorse Harry often told his students, "First you've got to be good, but then you've got to be lucky."

Golf Defined

Casual Water

Temporary standing water from excessive rain or flooding is known as casual water. A player may take a drop out of casual water and place the ball on dry ground no closer to the hole, and without penalty. This differs from a water hazard that is part of the course—in that case a penalty stroke is invoked after plopping a ball into the drink. (For more on that, see Chapter 12.)

QUOTABLE

"Why am I using a new putter? Because the old one didn't float too well."

—*Craig Stadler, PGA veteran*

WHY DO SOME PLACES PLAY GOLF UNDER THE LIGHTS?

Playing outdoor events under the lights has initially seemed abhorrent for most every sport. Baseball teams were dragged one at a time into the night until every major league stadium had light by the late 1950s—all except Chicago's Wrigley Field, which held out until 1988. Since most football teams played in baseball stadiums at the time, lights were generally available for football (except for Chicago Bears games at Wrigley, naturally). Yet the NFL schedule did not allow for night games on a permanent basis until *Monday Night Football* kicked off in 1970.

Golf is the ultimate daylight sport. Many golf courses at dawn are often bustling with activity, as regular diehards tee off as the sun first slides over the horizon and the dew soaks the feet of anyone without a good pair of golf shoes. At the end of the day on the same course there will be a different group of diehards, sometimes just a single individual, still out on the course trying to get in one last hole before being completely enveloped by darkness.

A sad and little-known part of golf's nocturnal history was pointed out in William Miller's 1999 book *Night Golf*. This children's book illustrates—with artwork by Cedric Lucas—that playing golf at night under a bright moon was the only way many African-American caddies in the 1950s and 1960s could get playing time on the course at all-white country clubs. This was long before anyone seriously pondered putting lights on golf courses.

Daylight golf is a matter of practicality. Golf isn't played at a stadium, where lights can be trained on a few hundred square yards of real estate. Each hole at a traditional 18-hole golf course generally covers several hundred yards. And that's if you hit the ball straight. Night golf is impractical in many ways… unless a television network and the most popular golfer in the world are involved.

The first "prime time" golf event broadcast live was held on August 2, 1999, a contrived match play event won by Tiger Woods over David Duval at Sherwood Country Club in Thousand Oaks, California. The overnight rating for the Monday night match was a 7.4, almost a full point better than ABC expected and comparable to the weekend ratings for the U.S. Open and Masters. So between the success for the network and for Woods, who earned $1.1 million for a night's work

Getting a jump on tomorrow's round at Rancho Mañana in Cave Creek, Arizona.

(Duval likewise did all right with $400,000), more night golf matches were held. Nevermind that the floodlights cast long shadows on the green by the end of the match.

People watched, but it was not great theater. Even the Golf Channel, which broadcasts or discusses any golf event it can find, called the night exhibitions "hit-and-giggle golf under the lights." ABC wasn't laughing when the ratings kept sliding after initial success the first couple of years. It eventually became a twosome competition and had a pair of three-year runs at exclusive California clubs thus dubbed "battlegrounds": Bighorn Golf Club and The Bridges. Though it still drew better than regular PGA Tour events *without* Tiger Woods, the event ended after seven tries in 2005. Woods ended up winning four of the seven *Monday Night Golf* matches and taking home more than $3 million (a significant portion of each player's share went to charity).

While those posh California clubs paid for the privilege of bringing in lights and letting the golf continue even after the sun had set in the

West, courses with permanently installed lights are usually a bit more modest. Most courses that play under the lights are called executive courses—all par-3 holes. Less real estate makes it easier to light and easier to keep track of the ball, conceivably.

The reason some amateur golfers play golf at night is the same reason many fast food restaurants are open twenty-four hours: Some people just can't get enough. Others work too late to get a chance to play during the daylight hours. Or they live in places where it's just too hot during midday in summer to safely or comfortably get in a round. Just as driving ranges that installed lights found customers stopping by for a bucket of balls at odd hours, golf courses with lights can earn more by staying open at night—or hopefully at least make enough to pay off both the outdoor light installation and the electric bill.

What if there's no night golf course near you? Make your own.

Night Flyer is one of a handful of companies that makes glow-in-the-dark golf balls. The ball stays glowing for several minutes after contact—enough time to find it between shots. While the ball is glowing, everything around you is, well, dark. There are plenty of other products to enable you to hit the course in the dead of night. A golf outlet store in New Jersey had lighted electronic golf balls for $13 apiece. While that is almost three times the manufacturer's retail per ball price for an elite Titleist Pro V1, try finding a Pro V1 in the dark.

Two light-emitting diodes (LEDs) inside a three-layer construction ball enable the ball to light up for approximately 30 hours. They are reusable for multiple rounds and respond just like a regular golf ball—only it lights up upon contact.

The cost per ball is cheaper if you shop around on the Internet, but the most economical—and enjoyable—way is to buy a tournament package directly from the company. All you supply is the dark. Now for some tips for hitting the night links:

Teeing off: Place glowsticks on either end of the tee box, hang a bendable 22-inch glowstick around your neck—for safety and better sight—and, most importantly, activate your lighted ball. Balls light up in several different colors, which is handy if you are playing with a foursome—and yes, the green ball is a much brighter green than the color of the grass.

Choosing a club: You'll want to keep a glowstick tied to your bag or at least keep one handy to help with club selection. Even if you're the only group on the course in the middle of the night, there's no excuse for slow play.

Hazards: Ideally, it's best to mark bunkers and other hazards before you tee off. If you're making this up as you go, maybe you can employ a forecaddy (or take turns being one) and toss a couple of glowsticks near the trap before you hit.

On the green: If you've reached the green in regulation, in the pitch black, you're a good golfer. You might as well shoot for birdie while all the birds are sleeping. A glowstick attached to the flagstick will help in aiming—you'll want to leave the pin in the hole in this case (since playing at night is mostly for fun, maybe this one time you can look the other way for the two-stroke penalty for hitting the flagstick from the green). As for the hole, you can twist a glow stick into a circle and place it inside around the lip or inside the cup.

Playing in the dark is a little more casual. Nine holes and winter rules are generally the norm. If you're going to play golf at night—or just go night putting (with the daughter of the dean)—you might as well have a good time.

When the night comes, this ball is ready to play.

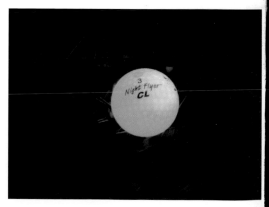

Hazards, bunkers, and wild Scottish grasses aside, Muirfield is a thing of beauty.

Did You Know?

Disc Golf

While throwing clubs is frowned on at any course, throwing is the name of the game in disc golf. The game has its own courses and approved plastic discs (don't be formal, call them frisbees). The Professional Disc Golfers Association credits the first practitioners as youths in Vancouver, British Columbia, using garbage can lids on a homemade course in 1926. It would be more than four decades later, following a failed commercial attempt by a company to market Sky Golf with plastic flying discs, that George Sappenfeld, while playing traditional golf, thought that the kids in the park he worked in would enjoy a frisbee version. In 1968, after he became Parks and Rec supervisor in Thousand Oaks, California, Sappenfield contacted Wham-O and asked them to provide materials that might get the game off the ground, so to speak. Though Wham-O sent the gear, and participants enjoyed this new version of the old game, it didn't catch on until Ed Headrick quit his promotional job at Wham-O and started the Disc Golf Association Company in 1976. Disc golf became part of Wham-O national frisbee promotional tour, introducing it to frisbee enthusiasts from all over the country. Disc golf took off and courses started popping up all over the country. Today there are about 3,000 estimated courses around the world. The chain baskets on poles may baffle some who come across them in parks, but when disc golfers see that they know their destination is at hand.

A disc golfer takes aim at a birdie chance.

Disc golf is fun for all ages—no clubs required.

Golf Defined

Divot

A divot generally refers to a slice of grass made when hitting an iron from the fairway. Etiquette requires that you pick up the missing earth and return it from whence it came, piecing together any scattered divot as best you can. Some courses provide a container on the cart with sand or a sand and seed mixture to pour over the sliced earth so new grass will grow there. Do whichever the course prefers—the presence of the jug with seed in it on a cart is a good indication—but it is necessary to make an effort because hitting out of a divot hole is no one's idea of fun. And carry a divot repair tool in your pocket to fix marks made by incoming balls on the green. Below is a little sign that is hopefully more helpful than a long explanation.

QUOTABLE

"Golf became increasingly harder for me. I shot in the 60s in the 1960s, the 70s in the 1970s, and the 80s in the 1980s."

—*Phil Rodgers, PGA pro and teacher*

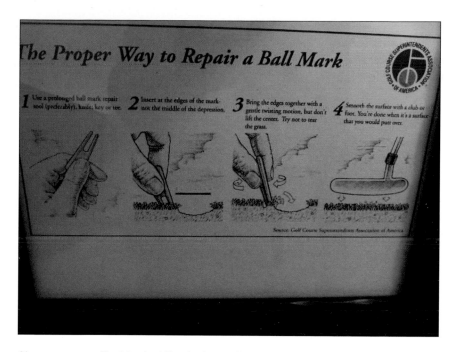

The Proper Way to Repair a Ball Mark

1 Use a prolonged ball mark repair tool (preferably), knife, key or tee.

2 Insert at the edges of the mark, not the middle of the depression.

3 Bring the edges together with a gentle twisting motion, but don't lift the center. Try not to tear the grass.

4 Smooth the surface with a club or foot. You're done when it's a surface that you would putt over.

Source: Golf Course Superintendents Association of America

Always carry a divot tool while playing golf—and know how to use it.

WHY DO THEY CALL IT THE RYDER CUP?

The Ryder Cup has been played every two years since 1927, though it missed a decade (1937-47) as a result of World War II. There have been changes in opponents, swings in dominance, and hurt feelings on both sides. Yet whenever the Ryder Cup is held, as it will be at Medinah Country Club outside Chicago in 2012, rivalries and differences are put aside as players vie for one of the 12 coveted spots on each team and then team up to try to bring the trophy home. American golfers consider it the highest honor as they can have in the game. Europeans, representing many different golfers from many different European nations come together to take on the Americans and try to claim the coveted Ryder Cup.

A match was held between Brits and Americans in Scotland before the 1921 British Open. The Walker Cup began the following year pitting amateurs from both countries against each other, but professionals sought a similar competition. Enter Samuel Ryder.

The Englishman had made a fortune in the seed business, selling seeds in individual packets. An avid golfer who didn't take up the game until age fifty, Ryder had suggested the idea of a match between professionals from the U.S. and U.K., at a time when professionals were often looked down on and were docked pay by their clubs for missing work to play in tournaments. Ryder and his trophy helped change that perception.

When a group of American professionals showed up a few weeks early for the 1926 British Open and played a group of British pros at Wentworth, the British won, 13½-1½. Luckily for the Americans, the trophy Ryder had commissioned was not yet ready. The match was considered unofficial, also in part because several of the players on the American team had been born in the British Isles. It was agreed that, henceforth, players would have to be natives of a country to represent it (this was later amended to citizenship).

Given a clean slate, the Americans got the first Ryder Cup in Massachusetts—ironically the same locale that the British had been rudely treated 150-odd years earlier in a skirmish of a different type in the "colonies." With Walter Hagen captaining a team that featured Gene Sarazen and Leo Diegel, America beat the British in 1927 on the golf course at Worcester Country Club, 9½-2½.

Home teams ruled the day for the first four Ryder Cups. The English pulled out a 6½-5½ victory at Southport and Ainsdale in Lancashire in 1933; it would be Britain's last triumph until 1957. The event moved around the U.S. every four years, with eleven different states hosting the next twelve events on American soil. The English moved the location around as well, but the result was the same. The American roster was stockpiled with legendary players. Just the names of a few of the U.S. captains who served multiple times creates a staggering list: Walter Hagen, Ben Hogan, Sam Snead, Arnold Palmer, and Jack Nicklaus. Nicklaus helped push for more competition and opening the competition to golfers besides those who called England, Scotland, and Ireland home. They got more competition all right.

After winning just once since 1933, the British were joined by players from all over Europe and their fortunes soon changed. The Europeans won twice in a row, including their first Ryder Cup victory on American soil in 1987 at Muirfield Village in Columbus, Ohio—Nicklaus territory with Nicklaus as captain. The competition became much more intense, as did fan interest in both the U.S. and Europe. Five straight Ryder Cups were decided by just one or two points, including a tie in 1989 (retaining the Ryder Cup for Europe since it had won the previous one). The Europeans rallied to win in 1995 at Oak Hill in Rochester, New York, 14½-13½. Europe won by the same score two years later in Valderama in Spain, the first Ryder Cup event not held in America or the British Isles. An unbelievable 45-foot putt by Justin Leonard sparked an impromptu celebration in 1999 in Brookline, Massachusetts, resulting in some hard feelings on the European side since José María Olazábal still had a 22-foot putt that could have changed the outcome. Apologies were later made by several Americans and both sides tried to tone down the growing nationalism in the event.

The two sides quickly agreed that the Ryder Cup was not a priority following the World Trade Center tragedy in September 2001. For the first time since World War II, the event was not held in an odd-numbered year.

The Ryder Cup returned in 2002 at the Belfry in Warwickshire, England, and the Europeans began their longest period of dominance, winning three straight times, including successive 18½-9½ victories in Michigan and Ireland in 2004 and 2006. The Americans ended that streak at Valhalla in Louisville in 2008, but the Europeans pulled out yet another one-point victory at Celtic Manor in Wales in 2010. The Americans still maintained the overall Ryder Cup lead at 25-11-2, but Europe held an 8-7-1 advantage since the field had been opened up to the continent in 1979.

Some pertinent numbers:
- 2: Ryder Cup ties, in 1969 (16-all) and 1989 (14-all)
- 6: Times that Walter Hagen captained the U.S. (1927-37).
- 8: Times that Americans Lenny Wadkins, Raymond Floyd, and Billy Caspar were named to the team.
- 11: Times that Nick Faldo appeared for Europe.
- 15: Largest margin of victory in 1967, by U.S. (23½-8½)
- 19: Age of Sergio Garcia (1999), the youngest European in a Ryder Cup.
- 21, 23: Americans Horton Smith (1929-31) and Tiger Woods (1997-99) were these ages for their first two Ryder Cups. (Woods was seven months older than Smith.)
- 23, 25: Most matches won and points won, by Nick Faldo.
- 46: Most matches played, by Nick Faldo.
- 51: Age of Raymond Floyd (1993), the oldest participant.
- 2016: Golf will become an Olympic sport for the first time since 1904.

Starting in 2016 in Rio de Janiero, golf will become part of the Olympics: a 72-hole stroke-play tournament for men and women, with 60 players in each field. It remains to be seen what Olympic golf will look like and what effect, if any, it will have on the Ryder Cup. The idea of playing golf for one's country has been at the heart of the Ryder Cup for eight decades. Unlike the rest of the PGA year, there is no money on the line, but for one weekend the players are not competing for themselves but for their country and for the game. The Ryder Cup is all that golf aspires to be.

Weighing four pounds and standing seventeen inches high, this solid gold cup is presented to the winning side in the Ryder Cup every two years.

It is not just the weight of responsibility on the shoulders of the golfers at the Ryder Cup—their caddies share the physical burden by toting these bags around.

Did You Know?

Thy Cup Overfloweth

Besides the Ryder Cup, there are numerous other cups doled out to teams of golfers who play high-stress match play tournaments with no payday, save for pride. Narrowing the field to four, these biennial events alternate locales, but in each event the Americans have the upper hand historically.

Presidents Cup: A shadow match of the Ryder Cup, professional golfers play this team competition in years the Ryder Cup is *not* held. The format is the U.S. against non-European competition. The 2011 Presidents Cup was won by the U.S. in Melbourne, Australia, giving the Americans a 7-1-1 mark since the event was founded in 1994.

Solheim Cup: American professional female golfers compete against Europe. The 2011 competition was held in Ireland and won by the Europeans, but the U.S. holds an 8-4 advantage since the inaugural meeting in 1990.

Walker Cup: The oldest of these competitions, its lineage dates back to when many still considered amateur golf superior to the professional ranks. American businessman George Herbert Walker, whose descendants would stay a dozen years in the White House, presented the first cup in 1922 to an American team led by legends Bobby Jones and Francis Ouimet, 8-4 winners over their counterparts from Great Britain and Ireland. Despite the home folks winning in 2011 at Royal Aberdeen, Scotland, the Americans still lead, 34-8-1.

Curtis Cup: A female version of the Walker Cup, it is held in even-numbered years. Like the Walker Cup, this is overseen by the USGA, and features the best amateurs from America against Great Britain and Ireland. The Americans hold a commanding 27-6-3 advantage following their 2010 win.

QUOTABLE

"Golf is neither a microcosm of nor a metaphor for life. It is a sport, a bloodless sport, if you don't count ulcers."

—*Dick Schaap, Author and broadcaster*

Golf Defined

'Fore!'

This is international golfing shorthand to watch out for flying balls. The term is believed to derive from British artillerymen warning friendly troops in front to "beware before," which was shortened to "fore." When you hear this yelled on the golf course, turn your head away from the direction of the shout. For heaven's sake, don't crane your neck toward the shout or you might wind up sucking wind and hearing Rodney Dangerfield's reply after his errant shot struck Judge Smails in the crotch in *Caddyshack*: "I shoulda yelled two."

ARE ALL THE BEST GOLF
COURSES PRIVATE?

Many people have the impression that to play a top notch golf course, you need to belong to a private club or know somebody who does. Those kind of connections don't hurt, but there are great public golf courses all over the country that you can play without breaking the bank.

Using *Golf Magazine*'s 2010 list of "Public Access Courses in the U.S.," there are 100 different courses covering thirty-five states. While some are pricey indeed, the magic number of $160 per round is used here as the dividing line between affordable and not so much. (Affordable is a relative term; there are countless courses available for well under $160—including some pictured here—and many resort courses have lower rates before and after the busiest parts of the season.)

Not surprisingly, California, given its massive size and golf-friendly climate, had 10 courses in the top 100, including a top 20 course Torry Pines in LaJolla, California, starting at $41 per round. The Golden State also has the lowest-priced round on the *Golf Digest* list: Rustic Canyon in Simi Valley, starting at $31 per round. Yet six top-ranked Cali courses are well on the other side of $160. The fabled Pebble Beach Golf Links is number two in the country in terms of play and price at $495 per round. (Shadow Creek in Las Vegas, ranked 17th-best among American public courses, nudges past Pebble at $500 per round on the *Golf Digest* list.) Spyglass Hill, another familiar public course on the California coast, has three holes listed among the PGA Tour's toughest; it fetches $350 per round. The best dollar per drive deal in Pebble Beach is The Links at Spanish Bay, at $260 per round.

Arizona had the best value, with all seven public courses on the list coming in at under $160. All six Oregon courses on the list are under that price, with four of those courses ranked among the top 15 public tracks. This quartet can be found on the Pacific Ocean in Bandon. The town of just 3,100 is about five hours south of Portland and in a world of its own when it comes to golf. All four courses have been constructed in the past dozen years, with a round at any of them starting at around $75. The *Golf Digest* ranking:

1. Pacific Dunes
5. Bandon Dunes
10. Old Macdonald

15. Bandon Trails

Hitting all four would make for some kind of weekend.

Just because a course is public, however, doesn't mean you can just stroll up with your foursome, or even solo, and hop on for a round. The public availability of these courses generally makes it that much harder to get a tee time.

Long Island's Bethpage Black State Park, the first "muni" to host a U.S Open (in 2002 and 2009), is among the most desired public courses in the country. As part of the New York State Park System, there are also Red, Green, Blue, and Yellow courses, but Bethpage Black, which does not even allow carts, sets golfers to drooling—or at least stocking up on balls.

Want to get on The Black? First you have to become a registered user. The line is long. There are 70,000 members in the reservation system and 35,000 tee times available in a given year. The best answer to getting on The Black has long been to bring a pillow and camp out in your car, though you can make reservations via phone a week in advance—non-New York residents can only reserve slots two days in advance. Phone reservations begin at exactly 7 p.m. Given that all available times are generally filled up by 7:03, this method of entry has been termed "impenetrable" by *Golf Digest* and by many who have tried it. Some have taken the extreme option of essentially "scalping" tee times through an outfit that charges up to $1,800 per foursome and $850 per single—that's about $10 per shot on the course, if you're on top of your game.

That is quite a markup for those who don't like to wait. New York residents who get on through less extreme channels pay $65 on weekdays and $75 on weekends (out-of-staters pay $125 and $135). But consider that the only way to get onto other New York City area private championship courses such as Winged Foot Country Club is to pony up in the neighborhood of $1,500 per person, if one can finagle an opening in a charity outing through connections.

Golf is about more than the cost, it's about the experience. Yet it's nice to know that of the 100 public courses on *Golf Digest*'s list, almost 75 percent of the courses have a greens fee starting at $160 or less. Half the courses available can be played for $100 or less. That's still a

Hitting from the fescue at Saratoga National in New York horse country. It may not be Bethpage Black, but it is a solid alternative available to the public for those who prefer a picturesque drive to sleeping in the car in hopes of a tee time.

lot to pay for a round of golf, but we're not talking about the pitch and putt down the road. These are the best courses in the country available to the public. What makes Bethpage so popular in New York—and even among those who fight the odds to get on as out-of-staters—is that it is accessible to all; there is no hefty fee for membership or a committee to meet and suck up to in the hopes of gaining social acceptance based on a criteria only vaguely understood by the upper crust membership.

"The People's Country Club" on Long Island is the antithesis of the secluded and restricted private golf enclaves that surround it. Bethpage Black isn't easy to get on or score on. The best things in life are often those which are the hardest to achieve.

Golf and farming come together with 27 public holes at Apple Greens, a functioning apple orchard in Highland, New York. Peachy!

Teeing off on 16 at the Tom Fazio-designed Ridgefield Golf Club in Connecticut.

Ocean Ridge Plantation, near the border of North and South Carolina, has multiple courses and tees for multi-level players.

Golf Defined

Immovable Obstruction

Players can take free relief from obstructions that cannot be moved. These are generally deemed as cart paths and maintenance roads on a course, but the rule also applies to temporary immovable obstructions as well, such as grandstands, tents, or even port-o-johns. The ball can be moved if it is in or on an obstruction, or is close enough so that stance or swing would be interfered with. The ball can be dropped no closer to the hole and one club length from the obstruction. If this happens on the putting green, the ball can be placed at the nearest point of relief no nearer the hole.

Grandstands, like these set up on 18 at Carnoustie for the 2007 British Open, fall under the temporary immovable obstruction category.

QUOTABLE

"I never wanted to be a millionaire, I just wanted to live like one."

—Walter Hagen, Golfing legend

HOW DID GOLF GET TO BE
SO POPULAR WITH ATHLETES
IN OTHER SPORTS?

Golf has a lot of things going for it that appeal to athletes. The game requires skill and precision, it creates competition on every shot as well as in the final tally, it provides the opportunity to show off and win "friendly" wagers, and, perhaps most appealing, golf offers infinite chances to rag on others.

Golf has a long history in attracting athletes from other sports. Unlike those who come to the game without superior athletic backgrounds, athletes are capable of picking up golf quickly, surpassing a layman's best score after just a few rounds. For many athletes who do not compete in their chosen sport for large chunks of the year, golf is a great way to stay active and socialize.

No sport has sent as many athletes to the golf course through the years as baseball. Even if most teams hope that players leave the clubs at home during the season.

Two all-time hitting greats were among the crossover pioneers of the marriage between baseball and golf: Ty Cobb and Babe Ruth. Though many of Cobb's career hitting records have been surpassed in recent decades, he has owned the mark for highest batting average for a century and counting. Ruth, who began his career as a stellar pitcher, converted to the outfield and held the career record for home runs from 1921 until 1974. Ruth is still considered by many to be the greatest player ever, which would surely irritate the irascible Cobb. Both were avid golfers. Cobb belonged to eight clubs, including the course friend Bobby Jones founded in Cobb's native Augusta, and the Olympic Club in Northern California, where the Georgia peach settled after his baseball career. A double Babe bill—Ruth and Didrikson (herself an Olympian turned pro golfer)—not only easily won a charity competition on Long Island in 1937, but the crowd was so large and exuberant that the Bambino was literally knocked off his feet by the surging crowd.

Another ballplayer from that era made a significant mark in the pro golfing ranks. Samuel Bryd was a Yankees teammate of the Babe's and was even called "Ruth's Legs" because of how frequently he pinch ran for the aging slugger. Byrd even followed the Babe out of town, with the Yankees getting rid of the reserve outfielder during the same 1934 off-season that they released Ruth. Byrd wound up in Cincinnati and

Ty Cobb had the highest batting average in baseball history using a famous batting grip where he kept his hands a few inches apart. As an avid golfer, though, the Georgia Peach kept his hands together when he gripped a golf club.

regularly got into the starting lineup for the first time. Byrd proved that he was no Babe Ruth. Byrd did outlast the Babe in the majors by a year, but the Georgia native was not yet 30 when he played his last professional baseball game in 1936. He had a second career on the PGA Tour.

Byrd won six PGA Tour events between 1942 and 1946. Though it should be noted that golf, like baseball, was missing its fair share of participants during that time due to World War II, Byrd did reach the PGA Championship final in 1945—when it was still a match play event—and lost to a pretty fair golfer in Byron Nelson. Byrd remains the only person to have ever appeared in both the World Series (his only Series game was in 1932 when he ran for—who else?—Babe Ruth) and The Masters (he placed third in 1941 and fourth in '42). A few others have tried their hand at both professions. Unlike baseball, if you don't win, the money is a lot harder to come by.

Rick Rhoden was a solid major league pitcher for 16 seasons, mostly with the Pittsburgh Pirates. He won 151 games in the majors and certainly could swing a bat, winning three Silver Sluggers at his position. He even served as the first pitcher to start a game as a designated hitter, batting seventh in Billy Martin's Yankees lineup on June 11, 1988. Rhoden's golf swing has also served him well, providing him another athletic career. He's won more than fifty times on the Celebrity Players Tour and his career earnings on the Champions Tour exceed $250,000. He has made the cut in two of the four Senior Opens he has qualified for.

Like Rhoden, some of today's best golfing ballplayers are pitchers: Adam Wainwright, Derek Lowe, Kyle Loshe, Tim Wakefield, and Justin Verlander. Livan Hernandez, who did not take up golf before fleeing Cuba in the mid-1990s, was still pitching in the majors in 2011 and is a scratch golfer.

So what is it with pitchers and golf? Yankee Derek Jeter, a shortstop who likes his golf, got in his dig in a 2010 article by Jack McCallum in *Golf Magazine*: "Pitchers show up to play golf every five days and play golf the other four."

John Smoltz, a 215-game winner, along with 300-game winners Greg Maddux and Tom Glavine, anchored the Atlanta Braves' rotation for 11 seasons. They also routinely hit the links, often bringing along a less permanent Braves rotation member to make it a foursome. Smoltz's belief is that golf made him a better pitcher. "I am convinced I would not have played twenty-four years without golf," Smoltz said. "They are both risk-reward sports, and you have to think only about the reward. Under the gun I don't feel any different trying to make a great golf shot than I do a great pitch."

While former Braves manager Bobby Cox had no problem with his golden trio hitting the links so frequently, other skippers have not been so accommodating. Second careers and offseason pursuits are one thing, but many front offices have never been happy about their players hitting the links during the long rigors of the baseball season. Even today, several teams do not allow players to bring their golf clubs on the road. For all the riches lavished on Yankees ballplayers, even Jeter has to leave the sticks at home.

There is a belief that golf during the season tires out players when they might otherwise be resting or does more damage to their swings than an extended longball spree in an All-Star home run derby. Ballplayers, for their part, see the game as an outlet from the stress in their day jobs—or in this case, night jobs. Hall of Famer George Brett even used to golf with his hitting coach, the legendary Charlie Lau. "He always stressed that the baseball swing and golf swing were similar, just on a different plane," said Brett. Add 500-home run sluggers Mark McGwire and Mike Schmidt to the list of those whose baseball swings were not hurt by their scratch golf capabilities.

Baseball players don't have all the fun on the golf course. The similarities between a slap shot and tee shot allow hockey players to legitimately claim that their sport directly helps them in golf. And that's not just spouting the script from the film *Happy Gilmour*. Brett Hull, Marc Savard, Jamie Langenbrunner, John-Michael Liles, Mario Lemieux, and Mike Modano were all among the top 18 in a 2009 *Golf Digest* ranking of top athlete golfers.

Three football players made the top five, with Dallas quarterback Tony Romo leading the way with what *Golf Digest* estimated as a plus-3.3 handicap. Also with plus handicaps were Hall of Fame receiver Jerry Rice (+0.7) and former punter Craig Hentrich (+2.8)—like pitchers, there's something about kickers and golf. Former kicker Al Del Grecco has a plus handicap and now even serves as the golf coach at his son's high school in Alabama—he works with the school's kickers to boot. (Ahem!)

Quarterbacks always had more on their minds than kicks and drives, but they do have a patron saint of golf to look up to: John Brodie, who called signals for the San Francisco 49ers for seventeen years, spent fifteen years on the Senior/Champions Tour, earning more than $735,000 in his golf career and playing in two U.S. Opens. (He also managed to fit in broadcasting both football and golf.) John Elway, Dan Marino, Marc Bulger, Derek Anderson, Drew Brees, and Ben Roethlisberger aren't in Brodie's class, but they are among the top recent QBs on the links. Brett Favre may also improve on his 1 handicap—provided he actually stays retired from the NFL.

For all the hysteria caused by Michael Jordan's mid-1990s switch from NBA superstar to minor league baseball rookie, he's better on the links than he ever was on the diamond. Charles Barkley talks a lot of golf, but his game is nowhere near that of NBA contemporaries Penny Hardaway and Clyde Drexler. Low handicappers from others sports include tennis players (Pete Sampras, Mardy Fish, and Ivan Lendl), bowlers (Walter Ray Williams and Bruce Webber), winter Olympians (moguls skier Nate Roberts, speed skater Dan Jansen, and downhill skier Bode Miller), a 10-time world champion surfer (Kelly Slater), and let's not forget Erica McKenzie. She was Ms. Hockey in Minnesota and starred on the ice for the UM Golden Gophers. McKenzie won a state golf title and plays to a 2 handicap. Golf is, after all, an equal opportunity sport.

Tony and Tiger: Dallas quarterback Tony Romo and Tiger Woods share a smile during a 2009 Pro-Am at Congressional Country Club in Bethesda, Maryland.

Did You Know?

Hagen Plays Ball

Walter Hagen is credited with popularizing golf to the masses and raising the stature of professional golfers, but he almost went pro in another sport instead. The only son in a working-class family of five in Rochester, New York, Hagen learned the game as a caddy at the Country Club of Rochester. By his mid-teens he was moved into the pro shop, giving lessons to members. Being a golf pro at the time was far from glamorous or lucrative. Also renowned for his skill on the ballfield as a pitcher and shortstop, the 21-year-old Hagen cancelled a tryout with the Philadelphia Phillies in June 1914 to play in a golf tournament. Later that week he won the U.S. Open, the first of his remarkable 75 tournament victories—47 of them PGA events, an organization he helped found at age 23. Hagen won five PGA championships, four British Opens, and a second U.S. Open. At a testimonial dinner for Hagen in 1967, Arnold Palmer said that the event at the Traverse City Golf and Country Club "could be held in the pro shop if it weren't for all you did to help build the game."

Walter Hagen in 1914, when he was still quite the ballplayer. He wound up making the right career choice.

Golf Defined

Match Play

A player, or a team, earns a point for each hole won in match play. Though stroke play (or medal play) is generally the rule in professional tournaments, match play was the original method used to determine the PGA Championship (1916-1958) and it is still used in the Ryder Cup and other team competitions. Scoring in match play is decided by the least number of strokes per hole, with players halving a hole if they both record the same score. When the match is tied, it is considered "all square." Once a player is up by more holes than there are holes remaining, the match is over. A player winning on the 17th hole is declared champion "2 and 1," meaning he led by two holes with one to play.

QUOTABLE

"In baseball you hit your home run over the right-field fence, the left-field fence, the center-field fence. Nobody cares. In golf everything has got to be right over second base."

—Ken Harrelson, Former All-Star and (briefly) PGA pro

IF WOMEN CAN COMPETE IN
MEN'S TOURNAMENTS, CAN
MEN COMPETE IN WOMEN'S
TOURNAMENTS?

The Ladies Professional Golfers Association states that to participate on the tour and in LPGA events, a player must be a female. Although she doesn't have to be born that way.

Until recently, men who had undergone sex change operations were barred from competition by a requirement that competitors had to be "female at birth." That rule changed in 2010 when the LPGA was sued by transgender golfer Lana Lawless, who had been a former club champion—as a man. Lawless filed suit against the LPGA in San Francisco in October 2010, claiming that the rule violated California civil rights law.

Lawless, a retired police officer, changed genders several years earlier and was the 2008 women's long driving champion. The event was cancelled in 2009, and when the competition returned in 2010, the governing body for long driving adopted the LPGA interpretation regarding eligibility. Lawless was barred from defending her title. Lawless subsequently wrote to the LPGA asking to compete in a qualifying tournament and was refused. She filed suit against the LPGA in October 2010. The LPGA, the longest ongoing women's professional sports association in the U.S., dropped its rule stipulation two months later.

More than three decades earlier, Renee Richards changed from male to female at age 32 and successfully sued to compete in the Women's Tennis Association. Richards spent four years in the WTA from 1977 to 1981 and was ranked as high as 20th in the world. Though Richards obviously sympathized with Lawless, she told the *USA Today* that she was on the LPGA's side. "I can feel her angst at not being accorded every last bit of rights and privileges that she feels she is now entitled to," Richards said. "On the other hand, I'm not so sure I feel that she is entitled to the right of competing on the LPGA with other women, although I think in her case, it's probably just fine because she's 57."

Women have long competed against men in recreational golf, and in the past decade a handful of women have competed against men at the highest professional level. Nothing in the PGA guidelines states that one has to be a man to do so.

Anika Sorenstam became the first woman to compete in the PGA Tour when she played at the 2003 Colonial in Fort Worth, Texas. Sorenstam had publicly been mulling the idea and the Colonial was one of

Michelle Wie is considered one of the top women in the LPGA and she competed in PGA Tour events as well.

three events that offered her a sponsor's exemption to play. The most dominant player on the LPGA tournament at the time, the 32-year-old Swede had won four major championships and was the first woman to shoot a 59. Though she did not make the cut, Sorenstam was the first woman to participate on the men's tour in 53 years, but she was not the last.

Suzy Whaley became the first woman to win a PGA individual professional tournament, capturing the Connecticut Section PGA championship in 2002 and thus qualifying for the following year's Greater Hartford Open. She played from tees that were 699 total yards shorter than male competitors, but she played from the same tees as the men at the GHO. She missed the cut with scores of 75 and 78.

Michelle Wie became the youngest competitor ever in a PGA event, competing at age 14 in the 2004 Sony Open in her hometown of Honolulu. She shot a 66 in the second round and missed the cut by one stroke. The powerfully built Wie competed in events on both the LPGA and PGA Tour as a teen. She had several top 10 finishes in LPGA events, but Wie did not make the cut in any of the eight PGA events she entered.

The last woman to play on the PGA Tour before Sorenstam—and the last before Whaley to win a qualifier to make a tournament—was Mildred "Babe" Didrikson Zaharias. Already world renown for winning two gold medals and a silver in track at the Los Angeles Olympics in 1932, she took up golf at age 24, and practiced 10 hours per day. Three years after taking her first swing, she competed in her first PGA event, the 1938 Los Angeles Open. She was teamed with professional wrestler George Zaharias—they were wed 10 months later. She made the cut in three PGA events in 1945, the only female golfer to ever do so. Zaharias won 17 consecutive women's amateur events and after helping found the LPGA in 1950, she won 14 consecutive women's professional events.

Zaharias helped change the public perception of women in sports, especially golf. The links had once been considered solely a male activity and the private golf clubs a sanctuary where men escaped from their wives and families and did not have to worry about women being present and perhaps reporting back home about their activities at the club. Men played the game, dallied over post-golf cocktails, suppered at the club, and came home when they were ready. Some clubs did not permit women to play golf, restricting dining rooms and lounges as well as golf facilities for men only. Many clubs have changed their policies in recent decades, some due to pressure or bad press. A handful of clubs remain restricted to women, with Augusta National the best-known club that does not allow female members.

The attitude against women golfing goes back more than a century. The popular feeling toward women playing golf during the sport's post-World War I craze is reflected in the classic satire *Babbitt* by Sinclair Lewis, written in 1924. George Babbitt shows a comely widow around the fictional town of Zenith. The woman, Tanis Judique, begins the sex-deprecating dialogue.

"Oh, of course, these women that try to imitate men, and play golf and everything, and ruin their complexions and spoil their hands!"

"That's so. I never did like these mannish females."

"I mean—of course, I admire them, dreadfully, and I feel so weak and useless beside them."

"Oh, rats now! I bet you play the piano like a wiz."

Physical competition among women was discouraged as it was feared this would make women "less feminine." Women's golf—fictional characters aside—did have its enthusiasts. The U.S. Women's Amateur was held for the first time in 1896 and the first Olympic medal won by an American woman was in golf at the 1900 Games in Paris, when Margaret Abbott, an art student, recorded a 47 in the nine-hole competition. The first U.S. Women's Golf Open was played in 1946 and was won by Patty Berg.

But don't expect to see men on the LPGA Tour, unless they are no longer men. And they still have to qualify for the LPGA Tour. On the other hand, more women will probably try their hand at the PGA Tour. Some of the male competitors may not like it, but the organizers, sponsors, and networks carrying these events—especially for some of the stops on the Tour that generate scant interest with single-sex fields—enjoy the peaked interest that such a challenge brings.

A woman tees off in the Adirondacks in upstate New York in the early 1900s.

Did You Know?

Sweet 16

Lexi Thompson became the youngest player to win an LPGA event when the sixteen-year-old captured the Navistar LPGA Classic in September 2011. She showed her mettle, overcoming a couple of late bogeys in the final round to still win by five strokes in Prattsville, Alabama. Thompson won a check for $195,000 and a pat on the back from the previous youngest winner of a multiple-round LPGA tournament, Paula Creamer, who won her first event at eighteen at the 2005 Sybase Classic in New Rochelle, New York. Thompson's success at the Navistar wasn't a total surprise. Two years earlier she had been the leader halfway through the event—at age fourteen!

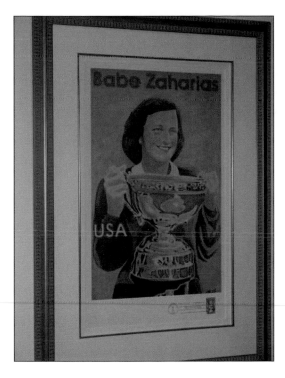

Babe Didrikson Zaharias was honored with a stamp in 1981. The painting used for her 18-cent stamp hangs in the PGA Museum.

QUOTABLE

"I just hitch up my girdle and let 'er fly."

—*Babe Didrikson Zaharias, Olympian and LPGA founder*

Golf Defined

Medal Play

Also known as stroke play, players compete against one another based on the number of strokes taken over the course of a round or several rounds. Strokes are either counted as they are taken or are modified according to a player's handicap. The term medal play derives from early golf in England, when medals were given to winners rather than trophies.

WHAT IS THE DIFFERENCE
BETWEEN WHITE, RED, AND
YELLOW STAKES ON
A GOLF COURSE?

In the life of every golfer a ball will cross a staked area. That is not good. But if that's where your ball went, them's the breaks. How bad the breaks are depends on whether your ball landed behind a stake that's white, red, or yellow. Here's what you're in for.

White Stakes

A chair just whizzed by from the gallery at the mere mention of white stakes. This is the least popular colored stake of the three. Some would even declare white stakes to be unnecessary in many cases. White stakes are arguably the most severe penalty in golf and one of the most controversial.

So what does it mean? A white stake means out of bounds—your ball has left the golf course. A lot of courses don't have white stakes at all, while other courses put them out to the extent you'd think a picket fence was following you around. White stakes are used by golf courses to separate course property from private property, to prevent golfers from crossing from one hole to the other to retrieve errant shots, or to delineate wild, wooded, or maintenance areas from the course itself. If your ball is one foot or one hundred feet past the white stake, the verdict is the same: You are in trouble.

The next question is, what do you do about it? If you are sure you have hit a ball past the white stakes, you must drop a ball and—as masochistic as it seems—hit the ball again from the same area where you just sliced/shanked/hooked/duffed your previous shot. The penalty is one shot and distance (since you aren't allowed to drop the ball where it went OB).

Your best bet, even if you think you might be able to find the ball, is to hit a provisional ball (make sure you inform your playing partner that you are doing so). If the original ball is indeed lost, you take the stroke and distance penalty. If you find your original ball and it is not beyond a white stake, then smile and stick the provisional ball—and stroke—back in your pocket. If you play the provisional ball anyway, that is considered playing the wrong ball, which is a two-stroke penalty.

If you find your ball in play near a white stake, you can stand out of bounds to hit the ball—as long as your ball is in bounds. You cannot,

Water hazards will even come for your ball in the desert. Notice the red and yellow stakes marking not one, but two ponds on this par 3 on the Cochise Course at Scottsdale's Desert Mountain.

however, move a white stake, even if it is in the way of your back-swing. And you can't take a free drop, either. As if golfers needed more reasons to detest white stakes.

Red Stakes

Kerplop! That's the sound of the ball going to its watery grave. The stakes on the border of the hazard are red. What do you do?

First, in the time it takes to go over to the area where your ball entered the water, calm down. You're still playing golf, you're not stuck in an office, and things could be worse—your ball could be on the wrong side of a white stake.

Compared to white stakes, red stakes are like a neighbor lending a hand in time of need. The red stakes mark a lateral water hazard, meaning that it runs alongside and not parallel to the direction of the green. To take a drop on the ground behind such a body of water could have you taking a boat across the other side of a river a thousand yards away. Even if it is just a creek or draining ditch, as long as it is marked with a red stake, you can assess a one-stroke penalty and take a drop within two club lengths from the point where your ball crossed the margin. It should be no nearer the hole than where it went in the drink.

And when you get to where the red stake is, you may even find that the ball is playable. You can hit the ball with no penalty, but when you play from a hazard you must not ground your club (placing the club on the ground behind the ball in address). In fact you may not touch anything. According to Rule 13-4 in the USGA Rule Book, you may not touch the ground or water with your hand or club. Nor can you move a loose impediment lying in or touching a hazard. Do any of these things and the red stakes suddenly become far less friendly with a two-stroke penalty assessed—or loss of hole in match play.

Yellow Stakes

Just like a stream running on the side of the hole can then cross in front of the hole, the color of the stakes can change as well. In the above example, that same body of water that had a red stake for your

The only birdie you're likely to find residing inside the red stakes is an egret.

If you are feeling lucky and can see most of the ball in a water hazard, try to hit it out . . .

slice into the water, may now be marked with a yellow stake as it juts in front of the green. If your ball lands in a hazard with yellow stakes, it's a different result, but the same one-stroke penalty. It's not stroke and distance like the white stakes, but hitting over the water again can be tricky, especially if it's a good-sized body of water that you just hit into.

Unlike the red stakes, however, where you drop a ball at the angle where the ball went in, it is dropped straight back, keeping the point where it went in between the ball and the hole. And then let 'er rip. (Again.) You can take the drop as far behind the water hazard as you like, even all the way back to where you hit your previous shot. But unless you're trying to relive the macho masochism of the climactic

. . . but beware of Barry Burn, which winds through the finishing holes at Carnoustie, where the 1999 British Open splashed away on the last hole.

scene from *Tin Cup*, take what the stakes are giving you and get as close as prudent to the spot where the ball went into the water.

If your ball is visible underwater, do yourself a favor, pick it up—or leave it be if it's hard to get to (or if it's in the vicinity of alligators!)—and take the stroke penalty and the drop. You should only consider going into a water hazard if most of the ball is above the water line and you can get it without having to take off your shoes. No one wants to recreate the image of Jean Van de Velde ankle deep at Carnoustie in 1999 after the Frenchman pitched into the Barry Burn on the final hole. He wound up picking up his ball and taking the penalty and the drop, but he still triple-bogied away a major and lost in a playoff.

Did You Know?

You Can't Knock Wood

Craig Wood held the U.S. Open title longer than any golfer in history. Born and raised in Lake Placid, New York, an area better known for turning out Winter Olympians than golfing champions, Wood in 1941 captured both Augusta and the U.S. Open at Colonial Country Club in Fort Worth, Texas. No one challenged his Open title for five years because the event was cancelled until 1946 due to of World War II.

Craig Wood, complete with tie, was one of the top golfers of the 1930s and 1940s and held the U.S. Open title for more years than any golfer in history—thanks to World War II.

UNDERWOOD & UNDERWOOD
WASHINGTON

Golf Defined

Mulligan

Just about everyone who's played golf in the last half century knows what a Mulligan is. But how did this term for teeing up a second—or third—ball after a bad tee shot come into being? The USGA gives several possible explanations, but the one that sounds the most likely is that the term was named for David Mulligan. A hotelier in the U.S. and Canada, he played at the St. Lambert Club in Montreal in the 1920s. After hitting a dreadful shot off the first tee, he impulsively pulled out a second ball and took what he called a "correction shot." His partners dubbed the term Mulligan after the originator, or so the story goes. Some people call it a "breakfast ball," others call it outright cheating. Call it what you will, but unless you're in a tournament or involved in a wager, let Mulligans be Mulligans and don't call someone on it that you don't call a friend. Worry about where your own drive goes.

QUOTABLE

"I know I am getting better at golf because I'm hitting fewer spectators."

—*Gerald Ford, U.S. president*

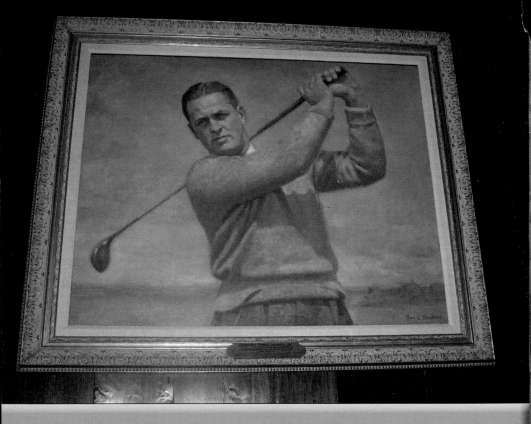

WHY IS THE FIRST MAJOR
OF THE YEAR CALLED
'THE MASTERS'?

The Masters wasn't The Masters its first five years of existence. The winners from 1934 to 1938 didn't win The Masters; Horton Smith ('34 and '36), Gene Sarazen ('35), Byron Nelson ('37), and Henry Picard ('38) won the Augusta National Invitational Tournament.

To make the tournament sound more prominent, the name was changed to The Masters in 1939. Bobby Jones, who founded Augusta National Golf Club with Clifford Roberts, disliked the new tournament name, thinking The Masters sounded pompous. The genuinely humble, Georgia-born Jones, a golfing legend and the founder of both the course and the tournament, relented on the point of the name. Ralph Guldahl was the first golfer to win the tournament under The Masters name in 1939.

Jones had originally petitioned the USGA to hold the U.S. Open at Augusta. The request was denied because it was thought that the sultry Georgia summer weather would make it too difficult for the players. Augusta settled on its own tradition, sending invitations to summon players to Augusta in the early spring. The first tournament was held at the height of the Depression in 1934, but a year later came its first taste of notoriety when Gene Sarazen recorded a double eagle on 15, known as "The Shot Heard 'Round the World" some sixteen years before that name became attached to Bobby Thomson's home run to win the National League pennant for the Giants over Brooklyn.

Sarazen came back to tie Craig Wood and wound up winning the 1935 tournament after a 36-hole playoff. Twenty-three years later, from the same location, Arnold Palmer drilled a 3-wood, cleared the stream in front of the 13th green and landed the ball 18 feet from the hole. He made the putt for eagle and wound up winning his first major. Bobby Jones, who watched both Sarazen and Palmer take their shots, said of the 1958 moment, "The same exhilaration came over me as when I watched Sarazen from the same mound in 1935." The feeling that Bobby Jones might still be watching, though he passed away decades ago, is part of the aura of Augusta National.

Starting in 1940, the tournament was set up to end on the second Sunday in April, a tradition based in marketing because many of the sports writers would be on their way north by train after baseball's spring training and thus could cover the tournament. The verdant course in bloom was matched by the green jackets worn by Augusta National members. Members had begun wearing the green jackets in 1939 so that patrons who had questions or needed help would easily recognize them. The tradition of awarding the tournament winner a green jacket did not begin until 1949, after the tournament had missed three years due to World War II. Sam Snead was the first player to slip into a green jacket after winning The Masters.

The winner could keep the green jacket for a year, but he had to return it to the club, where it was kept for him to wear when he returned to the grounds. It's a green jacket affair at the annual champions dinner the Tuesday before The Masters, open only to past winners and select few board members. When a new champion is crowned, the previous winner helps him slip on the jacket. That got a little tricky in 1966, when Jack Nicklaus became the first player to win the tournament two years running. Jack put it on himself in '66. (Future repeat winners Nick Faldo, 1989-90, and Tiger Woods, 2001-02, would have the club chairman to help them don the green jacket.)

Nicklaus was the third golfer to win the green jacket three times. Jimmy Demaret was the first (1940, 1947, 1950), followed by Arnold Palmer, the first four-time champion (1958, 1960, 1962, 1964). Nicklaus tied Palmer's feat in 1972, surpassed it in 1975, and stunned the golf world by winning his sixth in 1986, also making him the only man to win The Masters in three different decades. Other three-time winners include the first non-American to win at Augusta, South African Gary Player (1961, 1974, 1978), along with Nick Faldo (1989, 1990, 1996), and Phil Mickelson (2004, 2006, 2010). Tiger Woods, whose first win at Augusta set the course record at 18-under par and a 12-stroke victory, was victorious in 1997, 2001, 2002, and 2005.

Since Bobby Jones was the game's greatest amateur, The Masters has a strong tradition of amateur participation in the tournament. The field is made up of the previous year's winners of the U.S. Amateur and British Amateur, both of which Bobby Jones won during his unequaled Grand Slam in 1930. Jones won five U.S. Amateur titles to go with four U.S. Opens, three British Opens, and one British Amateur title, all of which were considered "majors" in his day (Jones didn't play in the

PGA Championship because he wasn't a professional). Jones only played in The Masters after he retired from competitive golf and never finished higher than 13th.

Each year at Augusta, the U.S. Amateur champion is paired with the defending Masters champion for the first two rounds. Also invited annually are the U.S. Amateur runner-up, and the champions of the U.S. Amateur Public Links, U.S. Mid-Amateur, and Asian Amateur.

Former winners of The Masters are invited to play each year, though the oldest are discouraged from competing once they have reached "advanced age" and are steered more toward the ceremonial events, such as the traditional tee off and par-3 tournament. The top 16 finishers from the previous year's Masters are invited back, as are the past five winners of the other three majors, plus the top eight finishers at the U.S. Open and the top four finishers at the PGA and British Open. The winners of the last three Players Championships are invited, as well as all players who qualified for it, the top 30 finishers from the previous year's PGA money list, winners of PGA Tour events since the previous year's Masters, and the top 50 players in the Official World Ranking.

Getting in field is almost as hard as getting tickets to watch the tournament in person. In 2011, for the first time in 47 years, a very limited number of tickets were sold by random selection, based on online registration. That's downright sporting and high tech for the tradition-bound tournament. Tickets have traditionally been sold only to longtime patrons of the club, so anyone hoping to break into the fold had better know someone or have plenty of cash to lay out. On a positive note, the pimento cheese sandwich was still only $1.50, at last bite.

The Masters is a worldwide event—in 1967 it became the first sporting event ever broadcast live overseas. It has survived war— Bobby Jones allowed animals to graze on the course during World War II—and it has weathered controversies regarding caddies (professionals were finally allowed to use their own caddies in 1982, though they still must wear white jumpsuits), African American members (that barrier fell in 1990), and women (Augusta National remains men only despite a contentious public snarl between Augusta's Hootie Johnson and Martha Burk in 2003).

Its one-of-a-kind layout features each hole bearing the name of a tree or shrub that has become associated with that hole. Most of the holes are slightly longer than Alister McKenzie's original layout, but the holes that are virtually unchanged are marked with an asterisk.

Hole	Name	Par	Yardage
1.	Tea Olive	4	435
2.	Pink Dogwood	5	575
3.	Flowering Peach	3	350*
4.	Flowering Crab Apple	3	205
5.	Magnolia	4	455
6.	Juniper	3	180*
7.	Pampas	4	450
8.	Yellow Jasmine	5	570
9.	Caroline Cherry	4	460
10.	Camellia	4	495
11.	White Dogwood	4	505
12.	Golden Bell	3	155
13.	Azalea	5	510
14.	Chinese Fir	4	440
15.	Firethorn	5	530
16.	Redbud	3	170
17.	Nandina	4	440
18.	Holly	4	465

The flower motif is another part of the tournament's charms, as is its placement just after college basketball ends, major league baseball begins, and buds just start to bloom again. Many a set of golf clubs is dusted off and shined up after a long winter following a viewing of The Masters on television.

Ten cabins on the grounds of Augusta National, available to members and their guests, lend yet more aura to the course and to the tournament that's simply called The Masters.

Did You Know?

Camouflaging

The architect of Augusta National was head of England's School of Camouflage during World War I. Dr. Alister MacKenzie had been fascinated by the art of camouflage since he experienced its effect firsthand as a field surgeon with the British Army during the Second Boer War in South Africa at the turn of the twentieth century. Bored with practicing medicine, MacKenzie became one of the world's most noted golf course architects, designing noteworthy courses on four different continents. His U.S. courses include Cypress Point, Pasatiempo, Meadow Club, Haggin Oaks, and Green Hills in California, the golf courses at Ohio State and Michigan Universities, Crystal Downs in Michigan, and Century Country Club in New York. But his lasting jewel is Augusta. MacKenzie became friends with Bobby Jones in the mid-1920s and the still relatively unknown architect was the legendary golfer's choice to design the course at Augusta. The property, which had supposedly been traveled by Spanish explorer Hernando de Soto in his search for gold in the mid-1500s, struck gold when it was transformed into a golf course. Augusta National formally opened in 1933, with a state-of-the-art underground sprinkler system, relatively few hazards, and 80 acres of fairway that was more than double the size of most courses... and twice as difficult.

Golf Defined

Play Through

Allow the group behind you to play through when it is clear that they are a much faster group. You may do it in the middle of a hole or before teeing off. It should also be considered when a group of at least half the size of yours comes up behind you, especially if the course is uncrowded. If only a single player is behind you, let the person join you or pass him through. It's all pretty basic stuff,

Another subtle hint to take notice the golfers around you.

but it's amazing how many people out on the course have seemingly never heard of the concept. So it's worth the explanation. If someone does let you play through, move quickly but not to the point where you have a lousy hole as a result. And say thanks.

QUOTABLE

"If there's a golf course in heaven, I hope it's like Augusta National. I just don't want an early tee time."

—*Gary Player, Three-time Masters champion*

WHAT IS A GOLF HANDICAP?

"**G**olf is my handicap" is a common reply to this question. That sentiment is certainly true in many cases, but the golf handicap allows golfers of different skill levels to compete against one another. A handicap is intended to show a player's potential, rather than simply his average score. And the United States Golf Association has been working on it for a century.

The handicap system has been a part of golf in America since 1911. It was revamped by the USGA in 1979—following scores of complaints (pardon the pun). The new formulas were in turn reworked in 1987 and again in 1993. The United Kingdom and Ireland have their own intricate system that requires software applications to calculate handicaps, but we'll let them be. The process of measuring the overall difficulty of golf courses, comparing individual golfers, and accounting for the differences between tournament and casual play in the United States is complicated enough.

Since you asked the question, let's break out the green eyeshades and dust off the adding machine.

To start, take your five most recent rounds of 18 holes.

Look up the slope and rating for the course(s) you played. These can usually be found on the scorecard itself. The slope at a U.S. 18-hole course is generally between 55 and 155; the higher the slope the harder it is. The average course slope comes in at 113. The rating, on the other hand, looks more like a golf score—a golf score by a really good player with a thing for decimals. The rating for a course is between 67 and 77. A higher rating means the course is deemed harder. Hence, a course with a par 72 that is deemed a little easier might come in at say 71.1, while one that plays harder could come in at 73.3.

Subtract the course rating from the score you earned on that course. Let's say you shot an 84 and for the sake of argument the rating happens to be a perfect 72.0.

Multiply the number by 113 (remember, that's the average slope). In this case it would be 12 x 113 = 1356. Well, that gives us a number that even the world's worst golfer could never shoot, so that's reassuring… and that number will go down soon.

Divide that number by the slope of the course. Who says we can't use 113 again? So we have 12 x 113 = 1356 and 1356/113 = 12. See what I did there? The number, 12 in this case, is called the differential.

Now take the lowest of the differentials from five rounds—we'll call it 12—and multiply it by 0.96. (Why 0.96, you ask? The belief is that this number is a "bonus for excellence," or an incentive to improve your game, since 0.96 results in a smaller reduction as compared to a high handicapper, giving good golfers a better chance of placing high in a tournament.)

What's your handicap? 12 x 0.96 = 11.5. So 11.5 is your handicap.

If only math—and golf—could be so easy.

The more scores you have, the more the calculation differs. So if you have seven scores, average your two lowest differentials and multiply by 0.96; if you have eight scores, take your two lowest differentials and multiply by 0.96; and if you have nine scores, average the three lowest differentials and multiply the result by 0.96. You can do that all the way to 20 scores. After 20 scores, use the most recent 20 scores and average the 10 lowest differentials, multiplying the result by 0.96 to get your handicap.

But if you are playing more than twenty times in a year, you really should have somebody do this for you. If you belong to a club, it will have a computer you can enter your scores in—but clubs can get rather pricey. You can join a men's or women's golf association at many municipal courses to help establish a handicap. It only takes ten members and a handicapping committee to become part of the USGA handicapping system. Then you can turn in the scores to the pro, log into a computer on site, or, a personal favorite, enter scores from your computer at home. The screen stares back the same way whether you've entered the best round or worst round of the year—that alone beats handing in the cards to a pro or having another golfer look over your shoulder and tap their foot as they wait to enter their scores.

The purpose of the handicap is to judge yourself against other golfers. Though if a stranger you've just been paired up with asks your handicap moments after asking your name, odds are he'll remember the number quicker than he'll recall your name.

Practice and dedication, regardless of age . . .

. . . leads to booming drives further on up the road.

The fourth hole at the renowned Fishers Island Club, on Long Island's eastern end, is known as "The Punch Bowl." With myriad ways to lose a ball on this devilishly beautiful par 4, it indeed packs quite a punch.

Every player is different and even players who arrive at a similar handicap number get there differently. We're talking about hypothetical based on an average golfer on an average course. The purpose of the handicap is to fairly pair up people in competition, whether it's an organized club tournament or a "friendly" $20 Nassau with the nail salesman next door.

Handicaps are tricky things, and it's not just the math involved. Some people like their handicaps high because they feel that gives them an advantage in tournaments and in general wagering on the links (see "Sandbag" definition). Others like to have as low a handicap as they can cheat—er, stretch—because they want to seem better than they are and quote a low number to impress friends and influence others. You do not want to be caught in the middle of these two schools of thought. Determining other players' handicaps is something you'd

Long Island civil engineer Seth Raynor, who built Fishers Island, worked with Charles Blair Macdonald to create the nearby Creek Club in Locust Valley, New York. The oak-lined third hole maintains that 1920s feel.

Though host of The Skins Game for six years, pros aren't overly fond of Pete Dye's TPC Stadium Course at PGA West in LaQuinta, California. No wonder. Earning a spot on the PGA Tour requires surviving qualifying school here. With a stroke rating of 76.1 slope and 150 slope, *Golf Digest* ranked it the fourth-hardest course in America.

rather stay away from because it can cause hurt feelings and you can get something else hurt.

In his book, *And If You Play Golf You're My Friend*, legendary golf instructor Harvey Penick told the story of a fellow pro he ran into at an airport. The friend had abruptly left a posh club to move to Florida to look for another job. Why the hasty exit? He had agreed to serve on the handicap committee at his club and in adhering to the numbers, wound up lowering a certain member's handicap by three strokes. It seemed harmless enough until the member caught him in the parking lot: "Give me my three strokes back. I've had people killed for less than what you did, pro."

Let's be careful out there.

Did You Know?

A Different Handicap

The handicap scoring system enables golfers of varying abilities to compete against one another. Golfers suffering from physical challenges can likewise take on the course and enjoy the game like anyone else. There are many different adaptive programs for golf. Some amputee golfers bring crutches and hit the ball by balancing on one leg, others hit from specialized one-person carts or from wheelchairs; those who cannot see play with the help of a guide who describes the layout and what the ball does after it is hit, and adaptive equipment can help those unable to grip a club, a tee, or a ball. The inclusion of golf in the 2016 Rio de Janeiro Olympics has led to a push for the sport to finally be included in the Paralympics, to be held in Rio shortly after the Olympics conclude. Yet it is the everyday disabled golfer getting in his swings and enjoying the outdoors with others that is the goal of the many organizations dedicated to this cause. Bob Buck, executive director of the Eastern Amputee Golf Association who has played with a prosthesis for decades and long maintained a 4 handicap, only sees the handicap printed on the scorecard: "If I'm playing against a guy who's got all his limbs and he's got a 14 handicap, I've got to give him seven strokes."

Steve Kave chipping at the 2008 Eastern Regional Amputee Championship at Bethpage State Park.

Golf Defined

Sandbagging

The art of entering a score that's higher than one should have earned in order to artificially inflate one's handicap and thus hold an advantage when competing against players with lower and more honestly arrived at handicaps. Among the origins for the term "sandbag," the most sporting comes from the world of horse racing, where dishonest handicappers, owners, jockeys, or stable hands would sometimes place bags of sand on the saddle to intentionally slow a horse's time. The traditional golf sandbagger may play poorly on one or two holes on purpose to inflate his score and increase his handicap. The subtle sandbagger may simply pay little heed to his score while out on the course; when asked what he got on a hole by the partner keeping score, he may call out "six" when he actually shot five. It all adds up.

QUOTABLE

"The most important shot in golf is the next one."

—*Ben Hogan, Golfing legend*

GOLF'S GREATEST RIVALRY

HOW DID THE RIVALRY
BETWEEN JACK NICKLAUS
AND ARNOLD PALMER BEGIN?

There have been great rivalries in professional golf: the amateur Bobby Jones against the pro Walter Hagen in the 1920s—with Gene Sarazen battling both as well; Ben Hogan fought fellow Texan Byron Nelson on the course, and when Lord Byron retired at the top of his game in 1946, Sam Snead became Hogan's top competitor; and in recent years there has been a lot of heat generated by the public and the media about Phil Mickelson against Tiger Woods. But no rivalry has meant as much to golf or its devotees as Arnold Palmer versus Jack Nicklaus.

Their rivalry helped fuel a golf explosion in the U.S. in the 1960s— and the duo's desire to play in the British Isles helped renew their countrymen's attitudes regarding the Open Championship. (Snead, who won the 1946 British Open and then did not play in the event for fifteen years, dismissed the travel and paltry purses: "Any time you leave the U.S.A., you're just camping out.") The Nicklaus-Palmer rivalry changed the way people followed golf, and the way it was covered on television. And their styles could not have been more different.

First came Palmer, the swashbuckling everyman with a loopy swing that would make a pro blush, bringing the masses to the game. Arnie constantly hit into trouble, hit out of trouble, and won and won and won. Nicklaus was more polished, growing up playing at a country club and developing a game that never had him out of place on any golf course against anybody, even as a seventeen-year-old amateur at the U.S. Open. By the time Nicklaus turned pro in 1961, Jack and Arnie already had a rivalry going. The star-studded, heart-stopping 1960 U.S. Open is where it began.

When he stepped to the first tee for the 1960 U.S. Open at Cherry Hills Country Club, outside Denver, Palmer had been a pro for six years. He had played golf at Wake Forest, dropped out of college, joined the Coast Guard, and after winning the 1954 U.S. Amateur, reluctantly decided to try his hand at playing professionally. Money was a lot harder to come by on the golf circuit in the 1950s, but Palmer proved he'd made the right decision by winning 18 tournaments in his first five years as a professional, including the 1958 and 1960 Masters. He would have won three straight at Augusta had it not been for meltdown on the last seven holes in 1959. Palmer hit two balls in the water at 12 and missed short putts on the last two holes to allow journeyman Art Wall to pass him with a stunning 66. Though gifted and popular, Palmer was not infallible. And he had plenty of competition.

Ben Hogan was a four-time Open winner and a legend. The gruff Texan's idyllic swing could still dissect any given course at age forty-seven, but his putting tormented him. Lucky to have survived a 1949 head-on collision with a bus, Hogan collected six of his nine major triumphs after the accident. He won all four majors at least once, a career Grand Slam achieved only by Gene Sarazen before him—and only Jack Nicklaus, Gary Player, and Tiger Woods managed the feat afterward.

Player, who would win nine majors, 24 PGA tournaments, and 166 professional wins around the world, was considered part of golf's "Big Three" in the 1960s and 1970s along with Palmer and Nicklaus. The South African was twenty-four in 1960—and he was the defending British Open champion.

Nicklaus was still in college in 1960, but he already had plenty of game. He had overcome a mild case of polio at thirteen in 1953, the same year he broke 70 for the first time. The 66 he shot at age fifteen was the record at his home course, Scotio Country Club in suburban Columbus, Ohio. He won five straight state junior titles and qualified for the U.S Open for the first time at seventeen. While at Ohio State he won the 1959 U.S. Amateur by sinking a birdie on the final hole and later that year helped America win the Walker Cup. Pudgy with a blonde crew cut, "Fat Jack" had visions of winning the U.S. Open as an amateur, as his idol Bobby Jones had. Nicklaus planned on becoming a pharmacist, like his father.

The 1960 U.S. Open was Nicklaus's fourth Open; he'd twice missed the cut and tied for 41st in 1959. He shot an even-par 71 in the first round in Denver, a tie for 12th with Ken Venturi and five others. The top amateur behind first-round leader Mike Souchak's 68 wasn't even Nicklaus, it was Don Cherry. No, not the hockey icon of Canadian TV, but the Texas-born singer who crooned out top ten hits and wrote the jingle for "Mr. Clean." Two pros missing from the first day leader board at Cherry Hills were Palmer, with a 72, and Hogan, whose 75 put him in danger of missing a U.S. Open cut for the first time since 1938.

Hogan got on track with a sizzling 67 on Friday, tying for 11th place with Nicklaus, Player, and Julius Boros. Souchak's lead, in the meantime, grew to three strokes after carding a 67. Palmer shot a 71 and was tied for 15th place with six others. As author Julian I. Graubart relates in his marvelous account of the 1960 U.S. Open, *Golf's Greatest Championship*, Palmer "was barely mentioned in second-round newspaper accounts. In a few articles, writers declared matter-of-factly that the pre-tournament favorite was out of the running."

All was to be decided on Saturday. The U.S. Open still finished with a 36-hole final day, which would be the rule until finally switching to a four-day tournament in 1965. Not only did this make it harder to televise (NBC provided trimmed-down, taped-delay coverage of certain holes), but the drama was also somewhat stifled by the pairing order (11 groups went out for the final round *after* third-round leader Mike Souchak). So in the nation's biggest golf weekend, coverage was hours behind "real time," and players were still coming in from the morning round while others were teeing off for the decisive afternoon round. Oh, but there would be drama in the afternoon.

Palmer's morning 72 left him seven shots behind Souchak and tied for 14th place with eight others. No one had ever come back from more than five strokes to win in the 56 U.S. Opens held since 1898—and since World War II, the biggest comeback had been from three strokes (Jack Fleck, ironically trailing by four after 54 holes in 1960, had made up three strokes in the last round in the 1955 Open to catch Ben Hogan, beating the Hawk the next day in an 18-hole playoff).

Palmer made a comment to a couple of writers in the locker room as he changed shirts and ate a hamburger, "Wonder what a 65 would bring this afternoon?" Palmer got only grins and a dismissive comment from *Pittsburgh Press* reporter Bob Drum, who had long followed the hometown hero from Latrobe, Pennsylvania.

Still angry on the first tee, Palmer got off a booming drive in the thin Colorado air that bounced on the green 355 yards away and started a legendary birdie flurry that turned the leaderboard upside down. Palmer birdied six of the first seven holes, hitting the turn with a score of 30 to tie the lowest nine ever in a U.S. Open (by James B. McHale in 1947).

Before Jack Nicklaus was even in high school, Arnold Palmer had already left college at Wake Forest and was serving in the Coast Guard. He continued to compete in the service but remained an amateur before finally turning pro at age twenty-five.

But the guy in the lead wasn't Palmer, or even Souchak—Nicklaus was in front with nine holes left.

Jack shot a 32 for the front nine, including an eagle at the fifth hole, to claim his first of many U.S. Open leads. Ohio State football coaching legend Woody Hayes appointed himself an acting marshal in the Nicklaus gallery and shooshed any who dared stir while OSU star Jack prepared to hit. Playing with stoic Ben Hogan, and battling him for the lead, Nicklaus felt intimidated enough not to ask an official about repairing a ball mark on 13 (which was within the rules). His putt from just a foot and a half away hit the indentation and missed the cup. Suddenly, five players were tied for the lead: Boros, Fleck, Souchak, Nicklaus, and Palmer.

Nicklaus, rattled for the first time all weekend, bogeyed again on 14. Now only Fleck and Palmer were tied at the top. Arnie was separated on the course from Nicklaus and Hogan by Gary Player, who stumbled home with a 76 to knock him to 19th. But for all the young guns shooting for the Open, it was the grizzled Hawk, Ben Hogan, who grabbed a share of the lead even as his agonizing putting threatened to undo an amazing run of 34 consecutive greens reached in regulation. Communication on the course was such—and his concentration so intense—that Hogan did not even know that it was Palmer he was tied with for the lead. When informed as much, Hogan responded, *"He's not a contender, is he?"*

Hogan laid up in two on 17, as did Nicklaus. Hogan went for birdie and the ball landed on the green, but backspin pushed it into the water. He took off his shoe—then put it back on without his sock—and hit out of the drink.

Hogan's bogey—and Nicklaus's par—left the pair thinking they had no shot at winning the tournament. Without updated leaderboards visible, players learned their fate from officials or fans who passed on information, and were not always correct. Both Hogan and Palmer could have birdied 18 and forced Palmer to make birdie on the last two holes. Hogan's tee shot hit the water—this time irretrievable—and he triple bogeyed. Nicklaus bogeyed. Palmer played it safe and sank a short putt on the final hole, firing his sun visor into the crowd in celebration.

Arnie had indeed shot his 65, bringing home a 280 for the tournament to set a U.S. Open record. Nicklaus placed second, his 282 an Open mark for an amateur. Hogan wound up tied for ninth place—the Hawk would never again get this close to his fifth Open title or tenth major.

Nicklaus and Palmer, on the other hand, were just beginning their rivalry. Nicklaus was married shortly after the Open in Cherry Hills, then returned to college, won an NCAA title, captured another U.S. Amateur, and—in an utter reversal of the average recreational golfer's dream—gave up his 9-to-5 ambitions to become a professional golfer. In 1962, in Arnie's backyard at Oakmont, Jack fired a 69 in the final round to catch Palmer, force an 18-hole playoff, and win the first of his record 18 majors. Between 1962 and 1969, Nicklaus posted 29 wins (seven majors, including the career Grand Slam) while Palmer won 28 times (three majors).

The rivalry burned white hot at times, reaching a boiling point when Arnie's Army openly rooted against Nicklaus at Baltusrol in the 1967 U.S. Open, but Jack shot a 65 on the last day to beat Palmer by four strokes. Tom Watson would become far more of a Nicklaus nemesis in the 1970s than Palmer, yet the public always relished the Jack-Arnie rivalry, even as both men moved away from playing and focused on golf club manufacturing and course design. The respect has remained.

In a 1994 *Golf Magazine* interview with the two legends, Nicklaus said, "Today, because of high tech equipment that minimizes errant shots, if a player hits too many shots offline, there are enough other guys out there hitting the fairways and greens and making putts that someone's gonna pass him. So there really isn't room for a personality like Arnold to show that exciting brand of golf—to come out of trouble and into the winner's circle."

Just like Palmer did at the 1960 Open. Golf hasn't quite been the same since.

Fifty years after they went down to the wire against each other at the 1960 U.S. Open at Cherry Hills, three masters—Jack Nicklaus, Gary Player, and Arnold Palmer—come together at Augusta National prior to the 2010 Masters.

Another legendary player who fought for the 1960 U.S. Open down to the wire was Ben Hogan. The Hawk has a room in his honor at the USGA Museum in New Jersey.

Did You Know?

Mini Golf

More often than not, a golf club is pressed into a person's hand for the first time—and for some, the only time—at a miniature golf course. St. Andrews has its claim in the genesis of golf, but it was also the locale of the first miniature golf course in 1867. Set up for ladies, scaled-down courses soon followed elsewhere. The U.S. was the first place it was taken seriously, though, with the Tom Thumb Open in 1930. Its $2,000 first prize was no small potatoes during the Depression. America was also where mini golf started moving—literally. In the 1950s the brothers Lomma—Ralph and Alphonse—began mass producing artificial greens, wagon wheels, windmills, and the like. Gimmicks helped catch the eye of passing motorists—and their families. The miniature game took off once more and tens of thousands of mini golf courses opened around the world, many of them climaxing with a final hole clown face that resulted in either a hole in one or a disappearing ball that forged the desire to pay for another round to try to win that elusive free game.

A person needs neither a fancy golf club to belong to nor a fancy golf club to swing with in miniature golf, the gateway to the game for millions.

Golf Defined

Stableford System

The Stableford Club in Yorkshire, England, is credited with devising a scoring system in which 5 points are awarded for eagle, 3 for birdie, and 1 for par, with subtractions made for scores over par. Most golf fans are more familiar with the modified Stableford system, used by the PGA Tour for The International at Castle Pines Golf Club in Colorado from 1986-2006. The modified Stableford doled out points as follows:

Score	Points
Double eagle	8
Eagle	5
Birdie	2
Par	0
Bogey	-1
Double bogey & up	3

QUOTABLE

"A kid grows up a lot faster on the golf course. Golf teaches you how to behave."

—Jack Nicklaus, Golfing legend

WHEN WERE AFRICAN AMERICANS FINALLY ALLOWED TO COMPETE IN TOURNAMENTS?

Though John Shippen was the first African American to play in the U.S. Open in 1896—and tied for the lead after the first day at Shinnecock Hills, where he was a caddy, before finishing fifth—it took until the 1960s for a black man to regularly play in Professional Golf Association tournaments, a decision that lagged behind the major American sports leagues, as well as tennis.

The other sports had kept African Americans out mostly through an "old boy" network, but the Professional Golfers Association had an article in its bylaws stating that membership was for men of "the Caucasian race." That language was removed in 1961, thanks to African American golfer Lee Spiller, whose long-running suit against the PGA came to the attention of California attorney general Stanley Mosk. He told the PGA it could not use public courses; the PGA replied that it would simply use private courses. When Mosk threatened to start contacting other state attorney generals, the PGA relented.

Sifford became the first African American on the PGA Tour when he teed up at Sedgefield Country Club at the 1961 Greater Greensboro Open. The golf tee Sifford used might have been the patented invention of the first African American Harvard graduate, George Grant in 1899, except that the successful Boston dentist never marketed his creation and only gave the tees to friends; a white New Jersey dentist, William Lowell, was the first to mass produce the idea with the Reddy Tee in the 1920s.

Sifford was thirty-nine years old when he became a PGA rookie, but he was a veteran of the United Golf Association. The UGA had been formed by African American golfers in 1925 in Washington D.C., six years after Negro League baseball was formed. The goal was to make golf equal for all and to create a means of support, both spiritually and financially. Affectionately known as "The Chitlin' Circuit," Sifford called the UGA "one of the greatest organizations in the world because it gave a lot of people a chance to play golf who didn't have anywhere else to play." Players from all over the country followed the circuit, and everyone wanted a shot at the annual Negro Open, an event Sifford won six times. UGA great Pete Brown recalled that it was called "a picnic" because so many people were on the course, some 200 or 300 would cram onto a course, including whites.

Though Sifford was the first African American to qualify for the PGA Tour, a decade earlier boxing great, Joe Louis, had been the first black to play in a PGA-sanctioned event—the 1952 San Diego Open. Louis also helped get seven African Americans a qualifying round for the Phoenix Open, a PGA event. Playing in the first foursome with Louis, Brown, and Eural Clark, Sifford recalled in his 1992 book *Just Let Me Play*, that he was so excited on the first tee he had to calm himself down after missing the fairway with his drive. He put his second shot on the green, in birdie range, and was about to pull the flagstick when "something seemed funny and I glanced down at the cup. I had the flagstick half raised but I shoved it back into the cup. Somebody had been there before us." The cup was filled with human excrement. Their concentration shattered, none of the men qualified.

Playing on the PGA Tour during the height of the Civil Rights movement, Sifford endured enough threats that he occasionally carried a gun in his golf bag. He won the 1967 Greater Hartford Open and two years later captured the Los Angeles Open in a playoff. Despite his PGA Tour wins and his standing among the top 60 money earners during his first nine years, he was still not invited to play in The Masters.

Lee Elder earned the first trip to The Masters by an African American in 1975. Three years earlier The Masters had gone to the format of including all PGA winners from the previous year, and he was tied for the lead after 72 holes at the 1974 Monsanto Open in Pensacola, Florida, the same course where Elder and other black PGA Tour members had previously been forced to change in the parking lot because the clubhouse was off limits. Elder won after a four-hole playoff to earn the invite to Augusta—not to mention an escort in a police car from the Pensacola Country Club clubhouse because of death threats.

Elder didn't make the cut at the 1975 Masters, but he heard cheers throughout his two rounds. He played there four times but the closest he came to winning was a tie for 17th in 1979. In 1997 Elder was in such a hurry to get to Augusta as a spectator that he received a speeding ticket. He did not want to miss Tiger Woods dominating the course. His 12-stroke victory lap at Augusta in 1997 was the first time an African American had won a golf major. Woods has since won the other three majors … at least three times apiece.

Though the "Tiger Woods craze" was good for golf, there has been no influx of young African American players joining the Tour who would have grown up idolizing Woods. Part of the reasoning, some think, is that the golf cart has replaced the caddie at all but a few select country clubs. Watching others play golf and being around the course has created some of the greatest players in the last century, of all races.

Programs like First Tee have provided young people and minorities with chances to play golf that they probably would not have had, reaching some five million participants since its inception in 1997. The pro ranks may not yet be filled with First Tee graduates, but progress in

At his peak, Tiger Woods was the most popular golfer — if not athlete — in America. A generation earlier he would have been hard pressed to be allowed onto some of the same courses he dominated.

the wake of the dramatic steps taken by Elders and Siffords and even Shippens may take time. Just creating more people who love the game, whether their aspirations are to turn pro or just break 90, is another step forward.

Did You Know?

Bill Powell's Clear View

Discrimination has never simply been restricted to the professional ranks. Besides caddies, who could play on the course when permitted (or when they would not be detected), African Americans were not allowed on golf club grounds unless they were performing manual labor or serving lunch. Bill Powell helped take care of that.

Powell, a returning G.I. from World War II and a passionate golfer who'd grown up caddying, wanted a place where he could play golf and not be discriminated against near his home in Canton, Ohio. Denied a bank loan, he received financial help from two doctors and one of his brothers and bought seventy-eight acres on a dairy farm. Doing the work himself during the day—he was a night watchman—Powell opened nine-hole Clearview Golf Club in April 1948, welcoming golfers of all races. Thirty years later Powell added another nine. Thirty-three years after that it was designated a national historic landmark. In 2009 the PGA bestowed Powell with its highest honor, the Distinguished Service Award.

Along the way his daughter, Renee, became the second black woman, after Althea Gibson, to play on the Ladies Pro Golf Association Tour. She played from 1967 to 1980 and went on to become head pro at Clearview.

The country's most exclusive clubs changed their discriminatory policies under pressure, notably Shoal Creek in Alabama, which admitted blacks after a firestorm of controversy prior to its hosting the 1990 PGA Championship. Other clubs that hosted PGA and USGA tournaments soon admitted small numbers of blacks to comply with the new code. But courses like that are out of the league of all but the highest rollers. Places like Clearview or Augusta Municipal, aka "The Patch," are where golf's everyman past—and maybe its future—can be found.

Golf Defined

Stimpmeter

The Stimpmeter is a device that measures the speed of greens. Edward Stimpson, the 1935 Massachusetts state amateur champion, was a spectator at that year's U.S. Open at Oakmont Country Club outside Pittsburgh. When a Gene Sarazen putt rolled off the green, Stimpson was convinced Oakmont's greens were extraordinarily fast. He set off to prove it by devising a 36-inch bar with a 145-degree V-shaped groove that is tapered to reduce bouncing. Balls are released at a 20-degree angle on a flat surface (a formula devised by A. Douglas Brede accurately gauges Stimpmeter results on sloped greens). Via the Stimpmeter, used by the USGA since 1976, come the following recommendations:

4.5 feet—slow green
6.5 feet—medium green
8.5 feet—fast green

Testing how the greens are rolling early on a Connecticut morning.

"GOLF - THE MOST FUN A COUPLE CAN HAVE IN PUBLIC"

Add two feet to each of the above numbers for the U.S. Open and you can see why par is often a winning score at the National Open. Oakmont, where the U.S. Open returns for the ninth time in 2016, regularly gets the old Stimpmeter running 13 to 15 feet. Edward Stimpson was right!

QUOTABLE

"The most rewarding things you do in life are often the ones that look like they can't be done."

—*Arnold Palmer, Golfing legend*

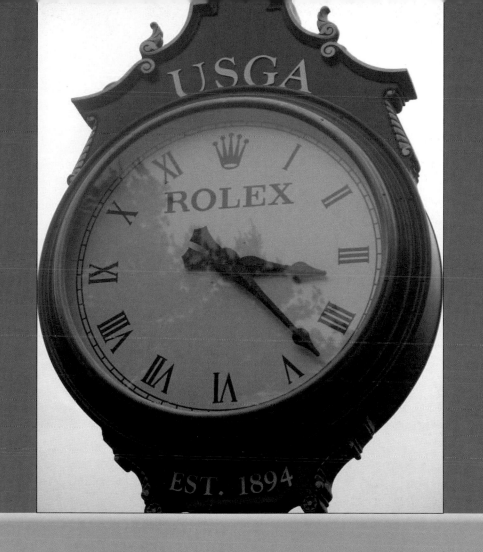

WHAT IS THE DIFFERENCE BETWEEN THE USGA AND THE PGA?

The PGA is for the pros. The USGA is for everyone else. For introductions, we'll start with full names: PGA stands for Professional Golfers' Association of America and USGA is the United States Golf Association. The organizations work toward the same goal of making golf as enjoyable as possible, but they have different missions.

The PGA is an organization of 28,000 men and women golf professional members, most of whom run shops and give lessons at courses throughout the country. In 1968 professional tournament players spun off a new organization, which officially became known as the PGA Tour in 1975. The PGA Tour runs 40-plus weekly tournaments, including the Players Championship, the FedEx Cup, and the biennial Presidents Cup, which pits American golfers against foreign-born players from countries beyond Europe.

So while the names have a similar ring to them, the PGA, PGA Tour, and LPGA are all different organizations. Each is headquartered in a different part of Florida.

In New Jersey, meanwhile, you'll find the USGA Museum and Arnold Palmer Center for Golf History in Far Hills. Known as "Golf House," this recently renovated building—originally built in 1919 by noted architect John Russell Pope—is bulging with the game's history. According to the USGA, the not-for-profit governing body "monitors the rules of golf

and equipment standards in an effort to ensure that skill rather than technology represents the essence of the game." The U.S. Open trophy is on permanent display in the museum in New Jersey. Each U.S. Open champion receives a replica of the trophy to keep permanently.

The USGA puts on the U.S. Open, the country's longest-running and most prestigious tournament. The inaugural tournament began— and ended—on October 5, 1895. The 36-hole event was held in a single day at the nine-hole Newport Country Club and won by club pro Horace Rawlins. A recent arrival to Rhode Island from England, Rawlins received $150 out of the $355 prize fund, plus a gold medal worth $50. A championship trophy was presented to the club by the USGA.

The USGA had formed less than a year earlier as the national governing body of golf. Organization was needed because two clubs deemed their club champion as the national champion in 1894. As we all know from more than a century's worth of annual debates about the number one team in college football, Americans like it when there is a single, undisputed champion. We like it even more when the champion shares our nationality.

Brits and Scots dominated the first sixteen U.S. Opens. John McDermott, who'd dropped out of high school in Philadelphia to become a professional golfer, rebounded from losing an 18-hole playoff in 1910 to win a playoff the following year at the Chicago Golf Club at age nineteen. To prove it was no fluke, McDermott won the U.S. Open again the next year, recording the first below-par, 72-hole score at a major championship (2-under par at the par 74 Country Club of Buffalo).

U.S. Open wins by countrymen Francis Ouimet and Walter Hagen established Americans as being on par with their counterparts from the United Kingdom, though no player would finish a U.S. Open with another below-par score until Bobby Jones was 1-under in 1929 at Winged Foot in Mamaroneck, New York. By then Americans held indisputable claim to the U.S. Open Championship Trophy—and, by the way, that is the name of the trophy, not Claret Jug, Ryder Cup, or corporate-sponsor-name-here trophy. And that U.S. Open trophy would not be won by a fluke. The USGA holds tight to a tradition that the Open is golf's ultimate test, with pinched fairways, jungle-like rough, and greens that push the Stimpmeter to the limit.

Between 1926 and 1993 only three non-Americans held the U.S. Open trophy aloft: South Africa's Gary Player in 1965, Brit Tony Jacklin in 1969, and Australia's David Graham in 1981. In that time, American legends Ben Hogan and Jack Nicklaus won the trophy four times apiece, equaling the marks set by Bobby Jones and Willie Anderson, the Scot who won four times in five years at the turn of the twentieth century. Of the twenty-one multiple winners, including three-time winners Hale Irwin and Tiger Woods, only two players from outside the U.S.—South Africans Ernie Els and Retief Goosen—have held the title more than once since McDermott broke the foreign stranglehold on the trophy a century ago. A recent trend has seen several foreign-born players win the U.S. Open. Northern Ireland sported back to back winners in 2010 and 2011 in Graeme McDonald and Rory McIlroy, respectively—the first consecutive winners from "across the pond" since the early 1920s.

The PGA of America was formed in the middle of a city in the middle of winter. The PGA dates its birth to a luncheon for the leading golf professionals and amateurs hosted by department store magnate Rodman Wanamaker at the Taplow Club in New York's Martinique Hotel on Broadway on January 17, 1916. Wanamaker figured that pros could increase sales of golf equipment with an association behind them. That October the first PGA championship was won by Englishman James M. Barnes at Siwanoy Country Club in Bronxville, New York. The 27-pound silver cup was—and still is—called the Wanamaker Trophy. More to the point, each of the thirty-two pros taking part were paid, with Barnes taking $500 of the $3,000 payout.

The PGA Championship was not held either of the next two years because of World War I (the U.S. Open and British Open as well as the Amateur Championships in both countries followed suit). Barnes successfully defended his PGA title in 1919 at the Engineers Country Club on Long Island. The next year Jock Hutchison, Scottish-born but an American citizen, claimed the PGA title. Walter Hagen became the first American-born golfer to win the title in 1921. Hagen would win five PGA Championships in all, a feat later matched by Jack Nicklaus.

Only two winners born outside the U.S. won the title from 1921 through 1957, when the PGA Championship switched from a match play to a medal play event. Some still long for the drama of match play, but the multiple matches needed to win—with 36-hole matches from the quarterfinals forward—made it grueling for competitors. The main reason for the change to stroke play, however, was television. Networks pushed for it and the perceived appeal of a wide-open field playing for the PGA title (as opposed to a one-on-one battle).

Since 1958, three Australians have won the Wanamaker Trophy (plus another won by Jim Ferrier in match play in 1947). Through 2011, no Brit had won the event since Barnes won the first two titles in the 1910s, but there have been repeat winners from South Africa (Gary Player), Zimbabwe (Nick Price), and Fiji (Vijay Sing). Recent winners have included Ireland's Padraig Harrington (2008), South Korea's Yang Yong-eun (2009), and Germany's Martin Kaymer (2010).

Yet while the public is most familiar with the U.S. Open and PGA Championship, there is more to the USGA and PGA than these two tournaments.

The PGA provides education and instruction for its members and hosts more than thirty events, including the Senior PGA Championship, PGA Grand Slam, and the biennial Ryder Cup that pits the top pros from America against their counterparts from Europe. In addition, the PGA Golf Club in Port St. Lucie, Florida, includes fifty-four public-access golf holes as well as a museum and learning center. The PGA has other golf properties in Florida and the Bahamas, as well as Valhalla Golf Club in Louisville, site of the 2008 Ryder Cup and the 1996, 2000, and 2014 PGA Championships.

The USGA administers several tournaments beyond the U.S. Open, including the biennial Walker Cup between amateurs from the U.S. and British Isles, the U.S. Women's Open, the U.S. Senior Open, plus the Men's and Women's Amateurs and Mid-Amateurs (the former open to golfers of any age with a handicap of 2.4 or lower and the latter for players over twenty-five with a handicap of 9.4 or lower).

The highest award the USGA presents is the Bob Jones Award in recognition of distinguished sportsmanship in golf each year. The award has gone to the biggest names in golf from initial recipient Francis Ouimet in 1955 to 2011 honoree Lorena Ochoa, who had retired a year earlier with thirty tournament wins before age thirty. Sprinkled among past Bob Jones Award winners were golf ambassadors/entertainers

The USGA's storied history is well-preserved at the historic "Golf House" in Far Hills, New Jersey.

Bob Hope and Bing Crosby as well as former President George H. W. Bush, who once played 18 holes in less than 90 minutes—golfing at the speed of light.

Golf's rules and championships are administered by multiple organizations with the same goal in mind: To make golf as accessible to as many people from as many different backgrounds and ages as possible. Yet golf is no longer the unstoppable growth industry it was a decade ago. The game must continue attracting new golfers and keep old ones coming back. Once someone gets hooked, they want to play every chance they get.

Visitors to the PGA Museum in Port St. Lucie, Florida, are greeted by the visage of Walter Hagen and the storied history of the professional game.

With the 2012 U.S. Open at the Olympic Club, the USGA has awarded San Francisco-Pebble Beach 10 Opens—and the only complaints are about the difficulty of the courses.

Did You Know?

Tiger Laps the Field

Tiger Woods set the all-time mark for largest margin of victory in a major with his 15-stroke win in the 2000 U.S. Open at Pebble Beach. His four rounds of 65-69-71-67 for a 272 tied the record for lowest score at a U.S. Open and was 12-under par, also a record. It was the first of three U.S. Open titles for Woods, tying him for second place with Hale Irwin. Willie Anderson, Bobby Jones, Ben Hogan, and Jack Nicklaus won the tournament four times apiece.

Golf Defined

Stymie

This term derives from the Scottish word "styme," meaning someone who is partially blind. Golfers used to be able to block an opponent's path to the cup by leaving the ball in the way— either accidentally or on purpose. This practice was abolished in 1952, much to the annoyance of many purists, including Bobby Jones. Players now mark their balls on the green, which allows the balls to be cleaned and whispered to for encouragement.

QUOTABLE

"The reason the pro tells you to keep your head down is so you can't see him laughing."

—*Phyllis Diller, Comedian*

The stymie once required skill and cunning to get around an opponent on the green. Now it requires a ballmark.

WHY ARE GOLF COURSES
18 HOLES IN LENGTH?

The Old Course at St. Andrews in Scotland is credited with the development of 18 holes for golf. Courses had however many holes suited the layout, or the men in charge. St. Andrews had 12 holes and players going out played the holes going out and then played the 10 lined up on the way back in, making a grand total of 22. It had long before been decided that it would be a waste to walk back carrying clubs and not playing.

Though some say golf was first played in the 1400s at St. Andrews in Fife, Scotland, the first proof of golf being played there dates to the mid-1500s. In 1553 the local archbishop issued a decree giving the locals the right to play golf on the links at St. Andrews.

In 1764, an order was given from the "Captain and Gentlemen Golfers present"—now known as the Royal and Ancient. These men were of the "opinion that it would be for the improvement of the Links that the four first holes should be converted into two—they therefore have agreed that for the future they shall be played as two holes, in the same way as presently marked out." The signature on the document, dated October 4, 1764, belonged to William St. Clair, four times captain of both St. Andrews and Leith golf clubs.

So the first four holes, which had been played twice per round—going out and coming in—were combined into two holes to make them longer, thus creating a round of 18 holes. Almost a century later, with golf growing more popular, St. Andrews put second holes on the greens, indicating which was which with a white flag for holes going out and a red flag for holes coming in. St. Andrews established 18 holes for matches between members. Other courses soon followed suit.

Initially, all the holes were doubled up. In 1863 legendary greens-keeper and professional, Old Tom Morris—the sobriquet was used to differentiate him from his son, the youngest winner of the British Open (seventeen) while his father was the oldest (forty-six)—separated the first hole from the 18th. This enabled the course to be played counter-clockwise, reversing the pattern used for centuries (that's why some of the 112 bunkers on the course seem to face the wrong way for unfortunate souls who land in them).

Today, the "Old Course" is played counter-clockwise, with the holes sharing a common green save for 1, 9, 17, and 18. And every hole has a name. Like so:

Hole (Name) Shared Green
1st (Burn)
2nd (Dyke) & 16th (Corner of the Dyke)
3rd (Cartgate Out) & 15th (Cargate In)
4th (Ginger Beer) & 14th (Long)
5th (Hole O' Cross Out) & 13th (Hole O' Cross In)
6th (Heathery Out) & 12th (Heathery In)
7th (High Out) & 11th (High In)
8th (Short) & 10th (Bobby Jones)
9th hole (End)
17th (Road)
18th (Tom Morris)

St. Andrews is still considered among the world's greatest courses. Jack Nicklaus said, "A British Open at the home of golf [is] the most intriguing and maybe the most demanding challenge in the game." Nicklaus won the Open twice at the Old Course, which has hosted the event 28 times since 1873 and is currently on a rotation as host every five years (ending with 0 or 5). South African Louis Oosthuizen won the Open at St. Andrews in 2010.

Yet the place could have been nothing more than a rabbit haven. When the town of St. Andrews went bankrupt in the early 1800s, rabbits were raised on the land and there were plenty of battles between golfers and farmers. But golfers in St. Andrews got their course back and have reaped the benefits. Locals did not have to pay to play the course until after World

Shadows join a fall foursome for the final hole of the day at Westchester Country Club's South Course in New York.

An old picture of the Old Course. St. Andrews in Scotland as it looked more than a century ago and many centuries after golf was first reported played there.

War II, in 1946. (The Old Course had been free to all until 1913.) The guest fee in the high season (mid-April through mid-October) now runs 130 English pounds (about $230).

No matter what you pay, people just want to play on the course where golf became what we know and revere today. St. Andrews is simply golfing heaven. Perhaps that's why the course is closed on Sundays, but you can still walk the grounds.

At North Berwick West in Scotland, hole 13 is simply known as "The Pit." And for all the tough lies on the course, the one below could be worse.

Lahinch in County Clare has been frequently referred to as "the St. Andrews of Ireland."

Royal County Down is both picturesque and as hard as a stone pillow. *Golf Digest* chose the Newcastle, Northern Ireland, links course as the best track outside the U.S.

The tree-size cactus species called saguaro does not require much water, but it seems to subsist on golf balls—at least these specimens at Desert Mountain in Scottsdale.

Did You Know?

Lord Byron's Eleven

Like Joe DiMaggio's 56-game hitting streak in baseball four years earlier, Byron Nelson's 11 straight PGA Tour wins in 1945 remains unchallenged. The Masters and the Opens in America and Britain were cancelled due to World War II, but the PGA Tour continued as public attention started to turn to pursuits beyond grim war news. Nelson, ineligible for military service because of a blood ailment, took part in countless golf exhibitions to raise money for the war effort. Nelson played in a PGA Tour team tournament with Jug McSpaden in March that began a streak that would place him among the mythic figures in the game's long history.

Miami International Four-Ball (team tournament)
Charlotte Open—shot 272, won by 4 strokes in 36-hole playoff
Greater Greensboro Open—271, won by 8 strokes
Durham Open—276, won by 5 strokes
Atlanta Open—263, won by 9 strokes
Montreal Open—268, won by 10 strokes
Philadelphia Inquirer—269, won by 2 strokes
Chicago Victory National Open—275, won by 7 strokes
PGA Championship (match play)
Tam O'Shanter Open—269, won by 11 strokes
Canadian Open—280, won by 4 strokes

A national sensation with his face on the Wheaties box, Nelson's streak finally ended in August with a fourth-place finish in the Memphis Invitational. Lord Byron won by 10 strokes the next week and finished with an unbreakable 18 Tour wins in 1945. He captured his last two events that year and his first two in 1946, a four-tournament winning streak exceeded by only two golfers. Tiger Woods won seven straight tournaments in 2006-07, plus streaks of six (1999-2000) and five (2007-08). Byron's rival, Ben Hogan, won six straight events in 1948, two years after Nelson retired at age 34 to become a rancher in his native Texas.

Golf Defined

Texas Wedge

In Byron Nelson and Ben Hogan's Texas of the 1930s and earlier, life was hard—and the greens were harder. A ball hit onto a rock-hard Texas green would generally bounce off, so players tried to land balls in front of the green so they could roll on and stay. When balls invariably came up short, a wedge might still knock the ball past the hole, so a Texas wedge—or putter— was prescribed. Texas greens have gotten a lot better, but a putter taken out to do the dirty work before the green still has its Texas moniker.

QUOTABLE

"I went to play golf and tried to shoot my age, but I shot my weight instead."

—*Bob Hope, Comedian*

The red barn on the ninth hole on Westchester Country Club's South Course has been a magnet for wayward second shots for generations.

A QUICK NINE

How Did Tiger Woods Get His Nickname?

This was a far more innocent question before the Tiger Woods extra-marital revelations, but let's just stick to the origin of the name of the world's most famous golfer, and the fact that if your name was Eldrick Tont Woods, you would embrace a nickname, too.

Earl Woods gave his son the nickname Tiger at a young age, just as he introduced the boy to golf, not long after he could walk. Earl Woods retired as a Lieutenant Colonel, serving in the U.S. Army Special Forces during the Vietnam War. He served as advisor to South Vietnamese Colonel Vuong Dang Phong, whom Earl nicknamed Tiger. Earl credited the original Tiger—or Tiger One—with saving his life from both sniper and viper in the Vietnamese jungle. The two men lost touch after 1971, but Earl vowed if he ever had a son he would call him Tiger.

Though Earl tried to find out what happened to the original Tiger, it was not until Tiger Woods became a golf superstar and international celebrity that the mystery was unraveled. *Golf Digest* reporter Tom Callahan went to Vietnam in 1996 to find out what happened to Tiger One. Callahan used the ruse of covering the 1996 opening of Nick Faldo's golf course in Ho Chi Mihn City, formerly Saigon, to launch his search. Callahan got nowhere, and was reprimanded by the Vietnamese ministry for not going through proper channels. While playing at Faldo's course, however, a businessman he met suggested placing an adver-tisement in Vietnamese-American newspapers asking for information. Callahan soon learned what happened to the original Tiger.

Tiger One surrendered to the Communists on June 15, 1975—six months before Tiger Woods was born. The colonel died in a re-educa-tion camp in 1976, though his family did not learn what happened to him for a full decade. Callahan also learned that Phong's widow, who had nine children, was living in Tacoma, Washington. She was completely unaware of who Tiger Woods was. A meeting was arranged in California between the families of the two Tigers: the colonel's widow and two of her children, plus Earl, Tiger, and Tiger's mother, Kultilda, whom Earl had met while in the service in Thailand.

Another Tiger Woods nickname, Urkel—after the quintessential nerdy kid on the 1990s show *Family Matters*—fell by the wayside by

In case the massive gallery and TV cameras wasn't enough of a clue, the Tiger head cover is a dead giveaway of who is coming up the fairway.

Arnold Palmer could do just about anything on the golf course, and the Palmer name became synonymous with the best clubhouse soft drink this side of a "Transfusion" (or ginger ale and grape juice).

the time he left Stanford University to turn pro. But another, happier nickname stuck with him. Earl Woods often called his son Sam as a boy—"because you look like a Sam." A year after Earl Woods died of cancer in 2006, a daughter, Sam Alexis Woods, was born.

Why Is Lemonade and Iced Tea Mixed Together Called an 'Arnold Palmer'?

Arnold Palmer is credited with making pro golf more appealing to the masses, transforming galleries into "Arnie's Army," and loyally following their man regardless of what was happening elsewhere on the course.

Anything cold to drink would be refreshing after putting around a bunker in the middle of the green at Jack Nicklaus-designed Chiricahua Golf Course at Desert Mountain in Scottsdale.

Palmer helped revolutionize the game with his daring, swashbuckling play, and he had the greatest player of his generation, Jack Nicklaus, as both a rival and a friend. Palmer has become a signature name, the face of golf, Pennzoil Motor Oil, and numerous other brands. All of this Palmer deserves credit for. How the mixture of lemonade and iced tea came to be named after him was more happenstance, but it does still speak of his popularity.

After a hot day designing a course in Palm Springs in the 1960s, the story goes that Palmer stepped up to the bar and made the order for lemonade and iced tea to be mixed together. A woman sitting at the bar immediately seconded the order: "I'll have that Palmer drink." News travels fast in Arnie's Army and soon the drink bearing the Palmer name was being asked for at country clubs, snack shacks, and even in nongolfing households across the country. Today Palmer's likeness is even on the beverage container of his signature drink. Those who like to spike their lemonade and iced tea with something a bit stronger are sipping "a John Daly."

A KING IS CROWNED

This display of Arnold Palmer at the USGA Museum, complete with wall hanging of him winning the 1960 U.S. Open, may be the only time one could say that Palmer went bust.

Why Is a Claret Jug Awarded to the Winner of the British Open?

The trophy for winning the British Open is essentially a jug used to serve claret, the dry French wine from the Bordeaux region. That's so very British—giving your country's most prestigious golf award in the shape of a fancy pitcher that serves a product made in another country.

Awarding the winner a belt, on the other hand, conjures up modern images of some renegade wrestling association handing out the prize to someone who hit six people over the head with a folding chair. But a red belt with a silver buckle was what was originally given when the Open Championship first started awarding prizes in 1860. Because the winner got to keep the Challenge Belt if he won it three years running, as Young Tom Morris—not to be confused with his father, Old Tom Morris, who won the first cash prize, 6 pounds in 1864—did, the tournament needed to come up with a new prize.

With the tournament changing from solely being held at the Prestwick Club to a rotation with St. Andrews and Musselburgh Links, a claret jug was agreed upon. A silver medal was also given in 1872 to Young Tom while the jug was still being made; the medal has been awarded to the winner ever since. The claret jug was completed by Mackay Cunningham & Company of Edinburgh. The cost was 30 pounds.

The original jug lasted through 1928 when a new model was awarded to Walter Hagen at Royal St. George's Golf Club. The winner must return the trophy after one year. At that time he is given a duplicate to keep. With an engraver on hand, the name is inscribed on the jug before it is awarded to the new champion. Mark Calceveccia opined as he awaited the trophy after winning the 1989 at Royal Troon, "How's my name going to fit on that thing?"

Why Don't PGA Players Ride in Carts During Tournaments?

Because the PGA Tour will not allow it—or the wearing of shorts, for that matter. The no shorts rule probably has saved many a gallery from "too much information" about players on the Tour. The no cart rule is a far trickier and thornier issue.

Old and Young Tom Morris won the British Open so many times between them—eight— that the championship belt was given outright to the son and a neat little silver jug was fashioned in its place.

The PGA Tour battled almost four years with Casey Martin, a golfer who suffered from Klippel-Trenaunay-Weber Syndrome, a rare circulatory disorder that left him with a withered right leg, and could one day face amputation. Martin stated that his debilitating leg condition made walking difficult and he needed the cart to compete. The Tour stated that it has a "long-standing requirement that the rules of competition be applied equally to all competitors."

The PGA Tour chose not to settle and lost the case in 1998. The U.S. Supreme Court upheld the ruling in 2001, saying that Martin's use of a golf cart would not fundamentally change the game. Although the USGA did win another case prohibiting Ford Ollinger, suffering from a degenerative hip disease, from using a cart in the 1998 U.S. Open in 1998, these cases weren't great public relations for a sport that already had a past filled with not-so subtle discrimination based on race and gender. To some people the cart issue seemed especially petty given that players in the early stages of PGA Tour qualifying school and members of the Senior Tour had access to carts. During a discussion of the case on ESPN's *Outside the Lines*, a tape was shown of PGA Tour players, including Tiger Woods, being shuttled to a hilltop tee in a minivan at a January 2001 event.

Jack Nicklaus, among others, spoke against the Supreme Court ruling, saying that walking was "fundamental" to the game. Many others agreed. Justice Paul Stevens, an avid golfer, did not. Stevens stated for the majority in the Supreme Court Case, "If the purpose of walking is to tax golfers' stamina, Martin's disability does that for him."

Martin, who briefly played on the golf team with Tiger Woods at Stanford, shot a 68 in January 2000 at the Bob Hope Classic while riding a roofless, one-seat cart allowed by judge's order while his case awaited appeal. Martin finished a career-best 17th at the Tucson Open a month later for his highest career payday: $37,950. He played in 29 tournaments in 2000, made the cut in 14, and earned $143,248. It was his only season with an average score below 70 and a spot among the top 200 money earners. He eventually lost his Tour card, but the Eugene native became the University of Oregon golf coach.

You have a better chance of being struck by lightning than winning the lottery. When thunder rumbles on the golf course, look for shelter back at the clubhouse or in a shelter built for the purpose like these two at the Whiteface Club in Lake Placid. Leave your clubs outside.

Keeping the greens watered at Pine Valley, Golf Magazine's 2011 choice as "Best Golf Course in the World."

Is Gamesmanship Ethical?

Well, that depends on whom you ask. In baseball, for example, "cheating" and "stealing" are terms for legal plays, but if every fielder who knew the runner beat the tag disqualified himself, many ballgames would end early due to a lack of players. In golf, on the other hand, professionals are expected to call fouls on themselves (as discussed in Chapter Six). But for amateurs, there is a much subtler way to manipulate their opponent. It is called gamesmanship.

At a 2010 panel at Duke University by the Kenan Institute for Ethics, "Bending the Rules: Gamesmanship in Sports," the term "gamesmanship" was defined as the idea that players can find new, risky ways of playing the game to gain an advantage. Jan Boxill, director of the Parr Center for Ethics at the University of North Carolina, cites gamesmanship as the root cause for the manipulation of rules in sports.

"Forty percent of [interviewed athletes] admitted to cheating and even more admitted they knew multiple people who cheat," explained Boxill. "It is about decency," Boxill said. "We all have the desire to win but, that doesn't mean . . . we must win at all costs."

This is all well and good in academia, but the layman's guidebook had been written some seven decades earlier. In a scant 128 pages, Stephen Potter's *The Theory and Practice of Gamesmanship* served as a primer for the subtle art of opponent manipulation without necessarily bending anything in the rule book. This tongue-in-cheek guide has maintained its popularity since it was first published in 1947—similar titles of Potter's have remained in print long after the Englishman's death in 1969.

Potter's *Gamesmanship* cites examples and provides illustrations (by Lieutenant Colonel Frank Wilson) on how to subtly get inside the head of opponents. The author uses games from snooker to croquet, but eventually the observant reader comes to the realization that he or she is being duped—Potter made up all the people and instances that he factually cites, even going so far as to include an index of his myths.

Once the reader realizes he or she is being duped, it enables Potter's peccadilloes to be better put into practice (or to be looked out for from opponents). Here are a few tenants from Potter:

- "Straight left arm at the moment of impact." Disguised as a compliment to a golfer on a tear, your opponent's shots will not be nearly as crisp once he is looking at his arm instead of the ball at impact.

- "Clothesmanship." Wearing the opposite outfit of your opponent. If he is smartly dressed, bring an extra set of clothes that are shabby or barely meet the course's dress code. (This went a longer way to rattling people in the 1940s.)

- "If he suspects you of being unsporting, extreme sportingness is the thing, and the instant waiving of any rule in your favor is the procedure." Getting called for messing with somebody is not something you want to do, but your obsequiousness may smooth over any ill feelings and inevitably work in your favor.

- "The way of the gamesman is hard, his training strict, his progress slow, his disappointments many." If your opponent has an A game and pays no attention to pathetic attempts at rattling, you'd best make sure you have enough cash to cover any wager. Or you could spend more time practicing shots than shooting down opponents.

Once upon a time, golfers wore jackets, made their own tees—and made their own luck. If they could get a little boost through gamesmanship, by gum they'd try it.

Caddies at Carnoustie are all smiles as they work at one of Scotland's finest links.

How Do You Play with a Caddy?

The Scots developed golf, and they also developed the caddy. Historians say the term comes from Scots not being able to say the French word "cadet," for young soldiers. This came up because Mary, Queen of Scots, who grew up in the French court, spent time playing

The starter calls down with assignments to the caddy house. No shack this.

the local game in Scotland and utilized her cadets in carrying her extra clubs. At least until she was beheaded in 1587.

In modern golf, few things can throw off some players more than going to a course that offers or requires a caddy. This generally comes up at select country clubs, especially on weekends or after heavy rains that make it unwise to send out golf carts because of potential damage to a saturated course.

When invited to someone's private club, bring enough cash so that your offers to pay can be backed up if your host takes you up on it. (See "Gamesmanship.") You should offer to tip the caddy for both you and the host if you can swing it, since guest fees at private clubs can be

Caddies at Westchester Country Club in New York watch from the tee on a par 3.

hefty. Tipping a caddy generally falls in the $50-100 range (per bag). If a caddy carries just the putters while the players take a cart—known as forecaddying—then $35 per golfer is more fitting. (These dollar amounts differ from club to club—you don't want your host to be known as a cheapskate because of your tipping.)

If this sounds expensive, think how much it would cost to play at the course—if it were open to the public—and also consider that the caddy is investing perhaps four hours in your round and may have to pay the golf course a cut of his share of the loop for the privilege of caddying there.

Don't blame your caddy for your bad shots or treat him like a lower class human being because he's carrying your bag. Some caddies have regular jobs and do a few loops to get playing time on the course. Others are up and coming golfers who might not only be better players than you, but their families may be members of this club. Caddies pick up a lot more on the course than just bags, and they might well know the game better than you.

Some tips (not of the money kind): Learn your caddy's name, say thank you, don't be a jerk, and listen to their putting reads if they prove accurate. But think twice about letting your caddy become your swing coach for a day if you're happy with your swing. If you have a preference, such as you like to tee off with a three-wood or three-iron instead of a driver on par fours or fives, tell the caddy early in the round since he will invariably head out a few hundred yards to watch your tee shot and bring your bag with him.

If you are not sure how much to tip when the round is over, ask your host. Asking the caddy master loudly in the presence of others may be seen as very Al Czervick of you, especially at a stuffy country club like Buchwood.

Why Isn't the Hole Larger?

Blame it on Musselburgh. It was at the Links of Musselburgh in central Scotland in 1829 where the first hole cutter was created with

If only a larger piece of drainpipe had been around when the first hole cutter was devised two centuries ago.

Twenty-year-old Francis Ouimet shows off the swing that transformed the former caddy into the 1913 U.S. Open champion and jumpstarted interest in American golf and the Open.

a converted piece of drain pipe, which happened to be 4.25 inches in diameter. A handle was affixed to the top and the holes could be screwed into the ground at a standard size.

When the Royal & Ancient Golf Club of St. Andrews set about standardizing the rules of golf in 1893, they went with the original hole cutter, which the Musselburgh Old Course Golf Club still has on display. Oh, for having a larger piece of pipe around the shed in 1829.

Why Do All the Majors Have Different Playoff Formats?

When a miraculous double eagle by Gene Sarazen set up a tie with Craig Wood in the last round of the 1935 Masters—then called the Augusta National Invitational Tournament—the pair played a 36-hole playoff to determine the winner. Sarazen won.

Masters founder Bobby Jones believed that 36 holes was the truest test of a champion. And for many years that's how it worked. Tournaments were often determined with 36 holes on the last day, the winner emerging from a grueling morning and afternoon round on Saturday. That it was done this way until the mid-1960s was tradition, but that it was done at all spoke of another tradition—members came first.

From the first U.S. Open held in 1898, the reason for the double-round finish was that the clubs wanted the prime days reserved for members. The first U.S. Open was held in one day, a Friday, with eleven golfers playing 36 holes, or four times around the nine-hole track at the Newport Golf Club on October 4, 1895. Of far more importance to the Rhode Island club's elite membership—besides the America's Cup yacht races, which postponed the Open for several weeks—was the inaugural U.S. Amateur. Held over a three-day span just before the Open, the 1895 U.S. Amateur was won by Charles Blair Macdonald, a Wall Street broker and pioneer in American golf course architecture.

For winning that first Open, Newport GC pro Horace Rawlins received a trophy, a few dollars, and a pat on the shoulder from a handful of members. This attitude was slow in changing. When the first U.S. Open playoff was needed in 1901 because of a tie between Scots Willie Anderson and Alex Smith, the pair did not tee off until Monday because Sunday was reserved for members at the Myopia Hunt Club in South Hamilton, Massachusetts. Anderson won the first of his four Open titles on Monday. Gradually the popularity of the Open became such that Sunday was reserved for a playoff if there was a tie after the final 36 holes on Saturday.

Thirty-three times through 2011 a playoff has been needed to determine an Open champion, from Anderson's 85 in the 1901 playoff for a one-stroke victory to Tiger Woods needing a 19th hole to beat Rocco Mediate in the 2008 Open playoff at Torrey Pines in LaJolla, California. Perhaps the most famous playoff, however, is still twenty-year-old American amateur Francis Ouimet beating overwhelming British favorites Harry Vardon and Ted Ray for the 1913 U.S. Open title at The Country Club in Brookline, Massachusetts, where Ouimet had been a caddy.

The Masters, established by amateur purist Bobby Jones, is now the only major with a sudden-death playoff. One bad shot—or one great shot from your opponent—and you're done. Fourteen times through 2011, Augusta has seen a playoff, with Gene Sarazen in 1935 being the only golfer required to play an extra 36 holes. Ben Hogan twice lost by a stroke in 18-hole Masters playoffs, while Byron Nelson, Sam Snead, Arnold Palmer, Jack Nicklaus, and Billy Casper all won 18-hole playoffs in Augusta before Fuzzy Zoeller became the first to win a Masters in sudden death, in 1979.

A quick denouement is optimal for TV networks as well as for reporters needing to scramble to alter travel plans and storylines in the event of an 18-hole playoff. There is a hybrid solution: an aggregate system, which is now used to determine both the PGA Championship and British Open in the event of a tie.

At the PGA it's the best cumulative score over three extra holes, while the British Open uses four holes. The TV networks like the minia-ture drama limited to an extra hour of coverage, as opposed to an extra day. But not everyone is a fan. Chris DiMarco, who lost playoffs in an

aggregate format at the 2004 PGA, and then on one extra hole to Tiger Woods the following April at The Masters, admitted to CBS, not surprisingly, that losing a major in just one extra hole was tougher to take. "There's too much pressure and too many weird things could happen. One hole is too much—or not enough, so to speak."

Even Woods, who has won in all manner of playoff scenarios, likes more time to determine the best man. "If I'm playing well, I want more holes," Tiger said. "Not just one hole, or even three."

How Are the World Rankings Determined?

Heading into the 2011 British Open in Sandwich, England, Luke Donald was ranked number one in the world and Darren Clarke was 111th. Neither had ever won a major championship. That week Donald struggled

at Royal St. George's, recording bogeys on the last four holes to miss the cut; Clarke, meanwhile, won the Claret Jug with a steady performance in ever-changing weather conditions. When the new rankings were released later that day, Clarke was $1.4 million richer and moved to number 30 in the world. Donald still stood at number one.

Both the numbers and public opinion were in accordance when Tiger Woods held the top spot in the world for the better part of 13 years, including a record 281 consecutive weeks from 2005 to

British golfer Luke Donald at the Heritage at Harbour Town Golf Links in Hilton Head. Despite being the top-ranked golfer in the world and highest-earning player in 2011, he did not win a major in his first decade as a professional.

2010. Since then, Lee Westwood, Donald, and a handful of others have held the torch, making the public wonder just how they came to be number one.

According to the Official World Ranking site:

> [Points] are accumulated over a two-year 'rolling' period with the points awarded for each event maintained for a 13-week period to place additional emphasis on recent performances — ranking points are then reduced in equal decrements for the remaining 91 weeks of the two-year ranking period. Each player is then ranked according to his average points per tournament, which is determined by dividing his total number of points by the tournaments he has played over a two-year period.

That's harder to read than some of the 80-foot putts on the massive greens at Royal St. George's. And it's harder for some people to swallow than America's Bowl Championship Series for college football.

Points come in many shapes and sizes in the world rankings. The system has been altered over the past quarter century, but its founder, Tony Greer, told *Golf Week* that he used to calculate the rankings "on the back of my hand." The current system awards golfers 100 points for winning a major, 80 points for winning the Players Championship, 60 points for placing second in a major, 40 for finishing third, 30 for fourth, down to 1.5 points for finishing all four rounds of a major. Varying point totals are given for other events on tours throughout the world.

The world ranking system was established by Greer, a British civil engineer, in 1986. Previously, the PGA Tour money list essentially served as the basis for setting the field for the major championships, but U.S. currency, among other factors, made it harder for foreign players to qualify. The international flavor of the world rankings was illustrated from the first day, April 6, 1986, when German Bernhard Langer was the first world ranking number one, followed by Spaniard Seve Ballesteros, and Scotland's Sandy Lyle. It took more than a dozen years for all four majors to exempt players using the world rankings. Once the Royal and Ancient endorsed the system for the British Open in 1997, the U.S. Open and PGA Championship followed a year later. The Masters finally acquiesced in 1999. The ranking also helps determine qualifiers for the Ryder and Presidents Cups, not to mention the Olympics starting in 2016.

Though the money list is no longer a determining factor in who gets the coveted spots in the majors and the prestigious match play tournaments, it's still about money. Endorsements contracts usually offer bonuses to players cracking the top 50 in the world rankings.

So as convoluted as it may seem at times, the world rankings keep the game more international and competitive—even if it often provides an unsatisfactory answer as to who is the best golfer in the world. That question is still answered differently at various watering holes throughout the world, long into the night.

Did You Know?

Saluting the Champion

After Payne Stewart died in a plane crash in October 1999, the next year's U.S. Open began with a 21-ball salute and two lines of forty or so PGA veterans hitting balls into the Pacific Ocean at Pebble Beach to honor Stewart, who had won the previous year's Open at Pinehurst. Chris Perry even wore Stewart's trademark knickers to salute his fallen friend. The early morning tribute was held at the 18th green overlooking Carmel Bay and the players were addressed by Stewart's widow, Tracy. "Even though Payne was fortunate to win the Open twice, he hoped to win it many more times," she told them. "No matter what the challenge, he never lost hope. He inspired us all."

When Tropical Storm Irene devastated Northeast hilltowns in September 2011, golf courses worked hard like everyone else to get back up and running. In New York's inundated Hudson Valley, courses didn't need power to open. Christman's Windham Mountain Course, Rondout, Catskill, and many others did not let up despite what was literally termed disastrous circumstances. The game must go on.

CATSKILL GOLF CLUB

Golf Defined

Unplayable

A ball can be deemed unplayable anywhere on the course, except in a water hazard. The penalty is one stroke. You can move the ball from the unplayable lie, but only within two club lengths—and not nearer to the hole than the original shot. Keep in mind, however, that if your ball is on an immoveable impediment, such as a sprinkler head or a cart, the ball can be moved off it without penalty within two club lengths no closer to the hole.

QUOTABLE

"Ninety percent of putts that are short don't go in."

—*Yogi Berra, Hall of Fame ballplayer*

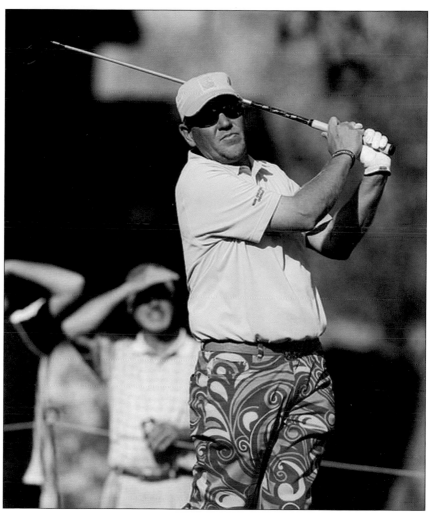

John Daly

PHOTO CREDITS